40 Poems for 40 Weeks

With this anthology of hand-chosen poems written by well-known, beloved poets, you can introduce poetry to your students in the classroom and beyond. Poetry is a powerful tool for teaching phonics, fluency, comprehension, vocabulary, and a love of reading. Curated specifically for students in Grades 3–5, this book contains 40 poems for 40 weeks in the school year, making it easy for teachers and librarians to read the poems sequentially throughout the year, choose them at random, or match a theme with current needs or events. The book eliminates the need to track down poems to read each week, and it provides a reading list of 120 books of poetry, making it one of the richest sources for poetry titles specifically for young students. Along with the poems are word ladders to aid in lessons on word decoding and encoding, vocabulary, and interest in word study. With poetry from award-winning authors and poets laureate, this is an essential resource for teachers and librarians hoping to inspire their students with poetry.

David L. Harrison is currently Missouri Poet Laureate. His 108 published titles include 90 books of poetry, fiction, and nonfiction for young readers and 18 educational books for teachers. His work has been anthologized in more than 200 books, translated into 12 languages, sandblasted into the Burton Barr Children's Garden sidewalk in Phoenix, Arizona, and painted on a bookmobile in Pueblo, Colorado.

Timothy V. Rasinski is a professor of literacy education at Kent State University, USA, and director of its award-winning reading clinic. He has written over 200 articles and has authored, co-authored, or edited over 50 books or curriculum programs on reading education. His scholarly interests include reading fluency and word study, reading in the elementary and middle grades, and readers who struggle.

Also Available from Routledge Eye On Education
(www.routledge.com/eyeoneducation)

Teach This Poem, Volume I: The Natural World
Madeleine Fuchs Holzer and The Academy of American Poets

Close Reading in Elementary School: Bringing Readers and Texts Together, 2nd edition
Diana Sisson and Betsy Sisson

The Antiracist English Language Arts Classroom
Keisha Rembert

The Literacy Coaching Handbook: Working With Teachers to Increase Student Achievement, 2nd edition
Diana Sisson and Betsy Sisson

What to Look for in Literacy: A Leader's Guide to High Quality Instruction
Angela Peery and Tracey Shiel

The Elementary School Grammar Toolkit: Using Mentor Texts to Teach Standards-Based Language and Grammar in Grades 3–5
Sean Ruday

Bolstering Vocabulary with Teacher Talk in the Classroom: Strategic Modeling to Elevate Students' Language
Kristen Haase and Carmen Shahadi Rowe

40 Poems for 40 Weeks

Integrating Meaningful Poetry and Word Ladders into Grades 3–5 Literacy

Edited by David L. Harrison and
Timothy V. Rasinski

NEW YORK AND LONDON

Designed cover image: © Getty Images

First published 2025
by Routledge
605 Third Avenue, New York, NY 10158

and by Routledge
4 Park Square, Milton Park, Abingdon, Oxon, OX14 4RN

Routledge is an imprint of the Taylor & Francis Group, an informa business

© 2025 selection and editorial matter, David L. Harrison and Timothy V. Rasinski; individual chapters, the contributors

The right of David L. Harrison and Timothy V. Rasinski to be identified as the authors of the editorial material, and of the authors for their individual chapters, has been asserted in accordance with sections 77 and 78 of the Copyright, Designs and Patents Act 1988.

All rights reserved. No part of this book may be reprinted or reproduced or utilised in any form or by any electronic, mechanical, or other means, now known or hereafter invented, including photocopying and recording, or in any information storage or retrieval system, without permission in writing from the publishers.

Trademark notice: Product or corporate names may be trademarks or registered trademarks, and are used only for identification and explanation without intent to infringe.

Library of Congress Cataloging-in-Publication Data
Names: Harrison, David L. (David Lee), 1937- editor. | Rasinski, Timothy V., editor.
Title: 40 poems for 40 weeks : integrating meaningful poetry and word ladders into grades 3-5 literacy / edited by David L. Harrison and Timothy V. Rasinski.
Other titles: Forty poems for forty weeks
Description: New York, NY : Routledge, 2025. | Includes bibliographical references.
Identifiers: LCCN 2024033797 (print) | LCCN 2024033798 (ebook) | ISBN 9781032785943 (hardback) | ISBN 9781032785936 (paperback) | ISBN 9781003489054 (ebook)
Subjects: LCSH: Children's poetry, American. | LCGFT: Poetry.
Classification: LCC PS586.3 .A14 2025 (print) | LCC PS586.3 (ebook) | DDC 016.8116/089282--dc23/eng/20240830
LC record available at https://lccn.loc.gov/2024033797
LC ebook record available at https://lccn.loc.gov/2024033798

ISBN: 978-1-032-78594-3 (hbk)
ISBN: 978-1-032-78593-6 (pbk)
ISBN: 978-1-003-48905-4 (ebk)

DOI: 10.4324/9781003489054

Typeset in Palatino
by KnowledgeWorks Global Ltd.

Access the Support Material: www.routledge.com/9781032785936

To Dr. Angela Knight, librarian
extraordinaire, who reads a poem every week
to the students at David Harrison Elementary
School and inspired this book. Thank you!
~ DLH

To all teachers and librarians who see the
value of making poetry an integral part of
their instruction
~ TR

The Purpose of the Book

The idea for this book was prompted by an elementary school librarian. You are about to meet her. She wrote the foreword for the book. School librarians support classroom teachers throughout the year. Our objective is to expand that partnership by providing librarians with enough poems written by many of today's best poets to share one poem a week to the entire student body (and supplement the poem with a wordplay activity that can be done in the classrooms or with the librarian in order to build students' vocabularies and word decoding abilities). In this way, librarians can ensure that all students are listening to and interacting with at least one poem every week and at the same time help teachers develop the habit of bringing even more poetry in their classrooms.

P.S.
If you are not a librarian, but a teacher or a principal or a parent or a student or absolutely anyone else who will take the time to read, respond, and share these wonderful poems with others, we're fine with that too. And we thank you for it! Promoting literacy and a love of poetry and words is a responsibility for all of us.

A Story Guardian

In a realm of wonder, where young minds take flight,
I stand as the guardian in the soft library light.
With eyes bright and hearts eager in their quest,
I nurture the love for learning, aiding each guest.

Amidst the shelves where colors and tales combine,
I foster dreams within books, a journey so fine.
Tiny fingers trace the spines, seeking treasures rare,
In the world of libraries, joy fills the air.

Whispers of giggles and the rustle of each page,
In the realm of picture books, where wonder's the stage.
An elementary librarian with stories to bestow,
Igniting imaginations, letting creativity flow.

Angela Knight, 2024

Contents

Meet the Editors... x
Foreword by Angela Knight............................xii

Introduction..1
Sylvia Vardell

1 **The Fun of Reading Poems Aloud** 4
   David L. Harrison

2 **Poetry and Word Games: Essential for Learning
   to Read** 8
   Timothy V. Rasinski

3 **Meet the Poets**.......................................11

4 **List of Suggested Books to Read**.....................207

Meet the Editors

David L. Harrison was born in Springfield, Missouri. Except for four years when his family lived in Ajo, Arizona, David grew up in Springfield, graduated from high school there (where he met and fell in love with Sandy Kennon, who would later become his wife), and graduated with a Bachelor of Arts degree from Drury College (now Drury University). Although he was a science major, David was told by a writing professor that he should become a writer. David went on to earn a Master of Science degree from Emory University in Atlanta, Georgia. He became a pharmacologist for Mead Johnson in Evansville, Indiana, but at night he began to write and submit his work. His professor at Drury turned out to be right. From that beginning in 1959 to now, David has published 110 books, including 91 trade books for young readers and 19 for elementary classroom teachers. His work has been widely recognized and awarded, including a Christopher Medal and A Pioneer in Education Award. He is poet laureate for Missouri as well as for Drury University. He has received two honorary doctorates in letters and David Harrison Elementary School is named after him.

Timothy V. Rasinski is a professor emeritus of literacy education at Kent State University. Tim grew up in Akron, Ohio. His first bachelor's degree was in economics from the University of Akron. After a three-year stint in the Air Force, Tim used the GI Bill to get a second bachelor's degree in elementary education. Tim taught in the elementary and middle grades of Elkhorn, Nebraska, where he was also a reading intervention teacher. After being encouraged by a professor in his master's degree program to pursue a doctorate degree, Tim went on to receive his PhD in literacy education from Ohio State. Tim taught at the University of Georgia before coming to Kent State where he directed Kent's award-winning reading clinic for struggling readers. Tim's research has focused on helping struggling readers in the foundational reading skills. In his research and work in the reading clinic, Tim found that poetry is one of the best texts for helping struggling readers improve their reading proficiency. Tim is an elected member to the International Reading Hall of Fame and in 2020 he was awarded the William S Gray Citation of Merit, the highest award given by the International Literacy Association.

Foreword

With immense joy and a profound sense of privilege, I pen these words as the foreword for my dear friend David L. Harrison and his newest poetry collection endeavor. David and I became fast friends as I began sharing his works with the students of his namesake school, David Harrison Elementary, in Springfield, MO. We have celebrated school openings, birthdays, Hall of Fame induction ceremonies, book publication celebrations, and the joy of reading with each other and our entire school community.

My excitement for this project is beyond my wildest imagination. It began simply as a conversation about how best to highlight David's work, a blog post, and then a math tangent. As guardians of knowledge and storytellers in our own right, we librarians hold the keys to unlocking everyone's imagination, and we constantly search for ways to engage our patrons and help them find their love of reading.

As the librarian at David Harrison Elementary and Holland Elementary, one (and sometimes two) of David's poems are read and enjoyed by the entire school every week of the school year. Our poetry initiative has rendered thousands of positive reading experiences, and the equation is calculated in this way:

> One poem each week for 36 weeks (Aug to May) times 576 students in the library every week equals 20,736 separate poetry exposures. These numbers are just the tip of the iceberg of what a poem a week can do for our hearts, minds, and souls. I have witnessed the thought, laughter, and pure joy firsthand.

Nestled within the heart of every library lies a treasure trove of poetry waiting to be revealed. Thanks to David L. Harrison's esteemed colleagues, Sylvia Vardell, Professor emeritus of children's literature at Texas Woman's University, author of such books as *The Poetry Teacher's Book of Lists* and *A Practical Guide to Children's Poets*, and current president of the International Board on Books for Young People; and internationally known scholar Timothy Rasinski, Professor emeritus of literacy education at Kent State University, director of its award-winning reading clinic on early literacy, and author of 100 articles and 50 books; plus 40 of the best wordsmiths publishing today, this anthology of elementary poetry and wordplay is a loving tribute to the magic of language and the boundless wonder it ignites in young hearts

So, to all the librarians, educators, and curious souls who call the library their sanctuary, or to anyone who has ever felt the pull of poetry, please immerse yourself in the pages of this collection. Allow yourself and your students to be carried away by the imagery, dance in the spaces between their lines, and find solace in their soul's echoes. In poetry, we find beauty, grace, and a mirror reflecting our humanity's myriad facets.

David, my dear friend, congratulations on publishing this new collection. Your words have touched the hearts of many, and I do not doubt they will continue to resonate for years to come. May this collection serve as a testament to your talent, passion, and soul's depth. I can't wait for my copy to be read at our school.

With love and admiration,

Dr. Angela Knight
Librarian
January 2024

Introduction

As adults, many people think of poetry as a rarefied kind of expression limited to the artistic, soulful few. Nothing could be further from the truth! Poetry is everywhere and surrounds us from our early childhoods with nursery rhymes and playground verse, fills our days as teens with song lyrics, rap, and text messages, and permeates our adult lives in television jingles, clever greeting cards, and even social media posts. We may not think of these communications as poetry, but they show us how everyday language can be rich, rhythmic, and poetic.

But if you work with children, poetry is even more important because it's a powerful vehicle for helping them develop their language skills. From an early age, children love the rhythm and rhyme of poetry and increase their knowledge of language and its conventions without even realizing it. When we think about developing phonemic awareness, the sound and rhythm of words and the importance of words' beginnings, endings, and middles, we see that is exactly what children learn by enjoying poetry. Their first exposure to poetry begins with lullabies, baby songs, nursery rhymes, riddles and wordplay, playground chants, nonsense rhymes, tongue twisters, jump-rope jingles, finger plays, hand-clapping games, and more. Children's book author and literacy expert Mem Fox noted, "Rhymers will be readers"; it's that simple. Experts in literacy and child development suggest that if children know eight nursery rhymes by heart by the time they're four years old, they're likely to be among the best readers by the time they're eight." These silly, simple rhymes lay the mental foundation for how literary language works as children learn to read and comprehend written text. Poetry does so much for children still developing their language skills and all in a concise linguistic package that can be shared out loud in just a few minutes.

Here's a quick list of the learning benefits of sharing poetry with children:

1. Poetry introduces new vocabulary and figurative language.
2. Poetry reinforces word sounds, rhymes, and patterns.
3. Poetry provides practice for word recognition and word pronunciation.
4. Poetry provides examples of synonyms, antonyms, puns, wordplay, and coining of new words and expressions.
5. Poetry often includes sensory language that communicates to children the senses of sight, smell, touch, taste, and hearing.
6. Poetry provides practice for oral language development, listening, and oral fluency.
7. Poetry has built-in opportunities for choral reading, group presentations, recitals, and performance.
8. Poetry has many pedagogical uses across the curriculum for building science concepts, reinforcing historical themes, adding motivation to math lessons, and as a quick "brain break."
9. The brevity and focus of poetry make it an effective tool for making cross-genre connections, connecting a poem with a work of nonfiction, a novel, or a picture book.
10. Poetry can heighten awareness of the use of mechanical conventions, from spacing and margins to commas and quotation marks.
11. Poetry offers an emotional connection and can reflect and elicit powerful and deeply felt moments.
12. Poetry is rich in imagery and in stimulating the imagination.
13. Poetry is accessible to a wide range of reading abilities and language learning skill levels.
14. Poetry is an important part of our literary and cultural heritage.
15. Poetry has a long shelf life, and poems can be revisited again and again, prompting different responses at different ages and stages.

The first step in inviting children into the world of poetry is very simply to read poems aloud. Hearing poems read out loud helps children attend to the sounds and rhythm of the words and lines as well as to their meaning. It sets the stage for children's participation in the read-aloud process. It familiarizes them with what the words of the poem should sound like and engages their listening comprehension in making sense of the poem's meaning. In addition, we can communicate to children our pleasure in poetry, in the sounds of words, in the rhythm of the lines. Through our willingness to share poems out loud, we subtly extend an invitation to children to follow our lead in trying poetry. The more children hear, read, say, and experience the poem, the more they internalize the sounds, words, and meanings of the poem and begin to notice the mechanics and artistry of poetry. As poet Brod Bagert has said, exactly as songs are not just sheet music, poetry is not just text. It comes alive when the words are heard as they are read aloud – the sounds of the words, the rhythm of the lines, and the space in between. The rhythm and rhyme of poetry can help children begin to get a sense of the sound of artful yet natural language. Plus, reading poetry aloud provides a common, shared literary experience that brings a classroom or campus together for a moment with everyone participating on a level playing field – all listening and responding to the same fun poem together.

In this wonderful new book, *40 Poems for 40 Weeks: Integrating Meaningful Poetry and Word Ladders into Grades 3–5 Literacy*, you'll find a rich resource to jumpstart your work with poetry with 40 featured poets, each with a contemporary poem for children, along with a photo and brief autobiography. Some of their many books are also referenced for further reading. In addition, Tim Rasinski provides a clever, innovative word ladder for each poem based on key words from the poem. With a fantastic poetry collection and resource like this, you are on your way to creating a culture of literacy, week by week, poem by poem. Let's get started!

Sylvia Vardell, PhD
Professor emerita, Children's Literature,
School of Library and Information Studies,
Texas Woman's University
Co-publisher, Pomelo Poetry Anthologies
President (2022–2024), IBBY (International Board on Books for Young People)

1

The Fun of Reading Poems Aloud

I realize that you who are reading these suggestions for presenting poems aloud are probably better at it than I and could teach me plenty. But I do have an excuse for thinking I might be of some help on the subject. When I write a poem, I hear in my mind how it flows along like a small brook, sometimes idling in a quiet eddy, while at others suddenly rushing headlong over sunken stones. Few poems, in my experience, are at their best when read as evenly as though a metronome was clicking off the beats.

I gave a poetry workshop one summer for teenagers. The poets had a tendency to be passionate about the subject, which was frequently about broken hearts. I required each poet to stand before the group and read their poem. One girl was so tormented by reading her work aloud that she stood in agony, drilling a hole in the carpet with one shoe, mumbling and stumbling over the words she had worked on so hard.

I alone, sitting so close to her, understood her poem. It was a good poem, but no one else in the audience got it and so the room remained quiet when the poor girl's torture came to an end. I stood and asked her permission to read her poem a second time. Nodding numbly, she handed me the sheet of paper on which her heart lay exposed and took her chair. I began to read the poem the way she had written it, with pauses for the listeners to follow and reflect as her meaning unfolded.

Around the room, an appreciative audience was taking this in. Kids were focusing on what they heard and understood. I observed a gangly boy on the back row. He had tears in his eyes. So did my poet.

At an International Elementary School in Kuala Lumpur, Malaysia, I paired a shy girl with a show-off girl to practice and read a partner poem to the rest of the class. The shy one had tried earlier to read something and was utterly undone, standing alone before her peers. Her words squeezed out in a whisper. But after practicing with a partner for a few minutes in the back of the room, we saw a different girl step up to the front, giggle at her partner, and perform with confidence. This time all the other kids heard and loved every word.

No matter how hard a poet has worked to construct his or her poem, it's up to the reader to present its meaning, depth, and beauty. The poet April Halprin Wayland set the responsibility to verse.

How to Read a Poem Aloud

To begin,
tell the poet's name
and the title
to your friend.

Savor every word –
Let
each
   line
      shine.

Then –
read it one more time.

Now, take a breath –
and sigh.

Then think about the poet,
at her desk,
late at night,
picking up her pen to write –

and why.

> Copyright © 2012 by April Halprin Wayland
> Used with permission of the author, who controls all rights.

One of the shortest poems I ever wrote, called "The Tick's Friends," is nine words long.

A tick has no friends, therefore, my story ends.

But in the book (*bugs, poems about creeping things*) it looks like this:

A tick
has
no friends.

Therefore,
my story
ends.

I read it that way too. A tick (pause) has (pause) no friends. Therefore (pause) my story (pause) ends.

If you are the librarian, teacher, principal, parent, or student who will be reading aloud the poems in our book, I hope you have a good intercom system. I hope you have a certain time of day when the sound of your voice coming over the PA system will not find kids at recess or in music class or engaged in other activities that need not be disturbed. I hope that after a short time, the students in your school will look forward to the short interval once a week when they get to meet another poet.

We have included a picture of each poet and asked each poet to tell something about themselves. This way you can read the short bio to your students and then the poem. You can show the picture and have fun with Tim Rasinski's word ladder based on the poem when you visit the classroom or the kids come to the library.

There are all sorts of ways to put this book to work at your school. You may be the only reader, take turns having guest readers, or do some choral reading. Practice is always important. I presented one of my own poems recently and butchered it. I hadn't rehearsed and was embarrassed at how poorly I read it. Just a reminder.

Thank you for using our book!

David L. Harrison, Litt.D.
Namesake for David Harrison Elementary School
108 published books for children and educators
Poet Laureate, State of Missouri, 2023–2025
Poet Laureate, Drury University, 1983–

2

Poetry and Word Games

Essential for Learning to Read

We are at a critical point in regard to literacy in the United States. Over the past 20+ years, despite enormous efforts by the federal government, states' school districts, individual schools, principals, teachers, and parents, we have seen virtually no progress when it comes to our children becoming fully literate. Indeed, a recent report by the US Department of Education found that about two-thirds of fourth-grade students are reading at a level either at or below "basic." So, what's the problem?

I feel that one of the major reasons for the continuing slump in reading achievement has been the development and implementation of an overly structured and regimented reading curriculum that allows fewer and fewer opportunities for teachers and students to explore the joy in learning to read. I am a firm believer that the best reading instruction is both based on science and is also artful. It's the artful part of that equation that has been left out. Teachers today are required to follow scripted curricula, to follow strict timelines, to focus instruction on improving test performance. When and how can teachers, and for that matter librarians, media specialists, reading coaches, interventionists, and school administrators, be educational artists?

Is it possible for reading instruction to be both science based and artful at the same time? I, along with David L. Harrison and the other contributors to this book, feel that the answer is a resounding YES! This book is one example of artful and scientific reading instruction. Let me explain.

Poetry, an artful text, is one of the most undervalued texts for teaching reading. The emphasis in the past several years has been on narratives (stories) and informational texts for building student knowledge. Poetry has been pushed to the sidelines. And yet poetry offers unique opportunities for reading instruction. Poems for kids are short, and full of rhythm and rhyme. These features make them ideal for teaching reading. Brevity, rhythm, and rhyme make poems easy to learn to read. (How many of us remember the words to poems that we learned in elementary school?) Children can experience success by learning to read poetry. Poems are meant to be performed. If performance is the end goal of learning a poem, then the poem needs to be practiced or rehearsed. Scientific reading research has shown us that repeated reading (i.e., rehearsal) is one of the most powerful ways for developing reading fluency and supporting word recognition (i.e., phonics). Poetry is filled with meaning that allows for the development of comprehension, unlike tests such as "Dan the man sat in a van with his fan on" that have minimal meaning. And, of course, poetry is joyful. Children love reciting and hearing poems. And let's remember learning should be fun! For all these reasons and more I think that poetry is the ideal text for learning to read, especially for elementary students and students who struggle with learning to read.

How many of us, as adults, like to play games such as Scrabble, Boggle, Wheel of Fortune, etc.? The answer I think is "most of us." We like to play games and so many of the games we play with family and friends are word games. If that is the case, wouldn't children also like to play word games? And the answer I have learned from nearly 50 years as a reading educator has been a resounding YES! And yet, compare that insight with current instructional word recognition programs that are marked by skill and drill that eventually come to turn many children away from reading. I am not saying that structured reading curricula are unimportant. What I am suggesting is that we need to find ways to incorporate authentic and engaging instructional activities within a structured curriculum. Word games are one way to do that.

Personally, I have always been fascinated with words, what they mean, how they are spelled, and how they are pronounced. I find it interesting that words can have many meanings, that they can spelled in a variety of ways, and that the pronunciation of words can vary quite a bit. I am also interested in how words came to be – many words have fascinating stories behind them. In short, I am what you might call a "lexophile" – someone who loves words. Being the word lover that I am, I also love to play word games by myself and with my family members and friends.

One word game that I have had a hand in developing is called word ladders. In a word ladder game, students are directed to go from one word to the next by adding, subtracting, or changing one or a few letters from the previous word. The game-like nature of a word ladder comes when students discover that the first and last words in the ladder are somehow related. In doing so, students learn insights into word decoding, encoding (spelling), and vocabulary (word meanings). Scientific research has shown that children doing word ladders on a regular basis demonstrate improvements in word knowledge and reading comprehension. In the present book, each poem is followed by a word ladder in which two key words from the poem are connected.

I (and my co-contributors to this book) feel that this book gives teachers, librarians, and other school professionals a tool for adding art-filled joy back into the reading curriculum, while at the same time keeping a focus on the science of reading. I sincerely hope that you give it your full consideration. It's a different kind of book. But in this age where reading achievement levels have been stagnant for so long, isn't it time to try something new (and artful)?

Timothy V. Rasinski, PhD
Professor emeritus, Literacy Education
Kent State University
Presidential Scholar
Top 2% Scientists Worldwide – Stanford University
2021 and 2023
Member, Reading Hall of Fame
Former Rebecca Tolle & Burton W. Gorman Chair in
Educational Leadership

3

Meet the Poets

The 40 poets you'll meet in the coming pages are some of the best and most beloved poets publishing their works today. A full list of all their awards would take pages. Among them are four recipients of National Council of Teachers of English (NCTE) Excellence in Poetry Awards, three Christopher Awards, one former U.S. Poet Laureate, one current state poet laureate, three former state poets laureate, two former Children's Poets Laureate, NAACP Image Award for Outstanding Literature, Coetta Scott King Award for Authors, one university poet laureate, one Newbery Honor, two Nebula Awards, one Sibert Medalist, three with books that won Caldecott Medals or Honors, and that is only a small sampling!

1. Alan Katz
2. Allan Wolf
3. Amy Ludwig VanDerwater
4. Avis Harley
5. Betsy Franco
6. Charles Ghigna
7. Charles Waters
8. David L. Harrison
9. Eileen Spinelli
10. Ellen Hopkins
11. Eric Ode
12. Georgia Heard
13. Greg Pincus
14. Heidi E.Y. Stemple
15. Irene Latham
16. Jane Yolen
17. Janet Wong
18. Joseph Bruchac
19. Joyce Sidman
20. Kalli Dakos
21. Karen Craigo
22. Kate Coombs
23. Kenn Nesbitt
24. Laura Purdie Salas
25. Lesléa Newman
26. Marilyn Singer

DOI: 10.4324/9781003489054-4

27 Marjorie Maddox
28 Mary Lee Hahn
29 Maryfrances Wagner
30 Matt Forrest Esenwine
31 Michael Salinger
32 Nancy Bo Flood
33 Nikki Grimes

34 Nile Stanley
35 Rebecca Dotlich
36 Renée LaTulippe
37 Sandy Asher
38 Sara Holbrook
39 Ted Kooser
40 Wyatt Townley

Our poets are listed alphabetically by first name. Each one is featured over four parts: a picture, a personalized biography meant to be shared with a young audience, perhaps a briefer "grown-up" bio, maybe a recommended book or two, a poem, for you to share with the kids in your school, and a word ladder created especially for the poem by Dr. Timothy Rasinski. In this way, students will get to know their poets as real people who were much like them when they were children. Becoming acquainted with the person who wrote what you are reading is a good way to build interest and empathy.

There is no "one way" to choose your weekly poet. Flip through the book and select a poem that pleases you for a particular day. The more fun you have, the more fun your students will have too.

Alan Katz

Something about Alan Katz

Hi! This is Alan Katz, and I'm so glad you're reading this book! To me, reading is the very best thing ever. To me it's even better than food. Why? Well, think about it this way: when you eat a sandwich, no matter how delicious it is, when you finish it… it's gone. But with a book, you can read it and enjoy it, and then… it's still there to be read again or shared with a friend. Make sense? I sure think it does.

I've been a reader and a writer since kindergarten, when Mrs. Gordon showed me the alphabet and said, "You can rearrange these letters and write words and use those words to make sentences and use those sentences to write a story or a poem." Or something like that. I started writing back then, and I've never stopped. (Actually, I've stopped to eat an occasional sandwich or two, but you know how I feel about that compared to reading.)

I'm proud to say that I'm the author of more than 50 funny books for kids, including four poetry collections and several picture books told in verse. I've also written nine Silly Dilly Songbooks, which are full of poems written to tunes you already know (such as "Stinky, Stinky, Diaper Change" to the tune of "Twinkle, Twinkle, Little Star").

I'm also proud of my family: my wife Rose is a Pulitzer Prize-nominated journalist; she writes serious stories that inform people about important issues. I write to make readers laugh, and she writes to share truthful information. But we use the same letters of the alphabet – that's the magic of words. I'm also proud of our four kids; Simone, Andrew, Nathan, and David are all extremely enthusiastic readers and writers.

Rose is also a very gifted poet, and her poems tend to be serious and thought provoking, whereas mine are meant to generate giggles. Some of my poems rhyme. Some don't. Some are based on things my family has experienced. Some come straight from my imagination (which I've been told is pretty wild). No matter which kind of poems are your favorites, I hope you'll enjoy *all* of the poems in this amazing book… and I hope they inspire you to write your own. Because you can. And you definitely should.

Now before you read my poem, here's a little more about me:

Alan Katz visits a ton of schools every year, and is a frequent presenter at regional and national conferences/festivals. He's received numerous state awards for his titles, notably *Take Me Out of the Bathtub and Other Silly Dilly Songs*, *Got Your Nose!*, *Zooloween*, and *Really Stupid Stories for Really Smart Kids*. Other recent titles include *Elf Academy: Trouble in Toyland*, three Lieographies (Babe Ruth, Amelia Earhart, and Thomas Edison), and the first five books in the Society of Substitutes series.

Alan is also a six-time Emmy-nominated writer for TV series including *The Rosie O'Donnell Show*, *The Tony Danza Show*, several Nickelodeon and PBS Kids series, and the animated shows *Pinkalicious*, *Taz-Mania*, and *Goof Troop*.

Alan also hosted a long-running game show on SiriusXM's Kids Place Live channel, and he's created comic books, trading cards, theme park shows, stage musicals (including *The Silly Dilly Musical*, based on his nine Silly Dilly songbooks), and hundreds of others special projects for kids and their parents.

Okay, now you know everything about me. Get ready to read my poem… then have a sandwich… then continue reading. I'll see ya!

A Poem by Alan Katz

The word "If" holds a world of incredible possibilities. I love starting a poem with that word and seeing where it takes me. Here's one that took me in a very unpredictable direction. I hope you enjoy it!

WINGS

If I could have one wish of all… I'd wish for wings.
Wings that would fuel me.
Nourish me.
And make my body soar with happiness.

Wings would help me to take on new challenges.
Who knows, after having wings, maybe I could change the world.

I think about having wings when I wake up.
I think about having wings all day.
I think about having wings as I fall asleep.

So, I say it now, and I say it clearly:
I would like wings.
What's that? You're out of wings?
Okay, never mind. I'll have the mozzarella sticks.

I plan to include this poem in an upcoming collection. Two of my other poetry books that I think might make you laugh are *Oops!* (2008) and *Poems I Wrote When No One Was Looking* (2011). Both were beautifully illustrated by Edward Koren and published by Margaret K. McElderry Books.

A Word Ladder by Timothy Rasinski

In a word ladder game, lead students from one word to the next by adding, subtracting, or changing one or a few letters from the previous word. Start at the top and work toward the bottom.

1 Wish	A desire or hope for something.
2 Dish	A plate on which food is served. Change 1.
3 Disk	A thin, flat, round object that is flat and round. Change 1.
4 Skid	To slide suddenly sideways as a vehicle that has lost traction. Rearrange letters.
5 Skim	A type of milk with no fat. Change 1.
6 Slim	Thin or slender. Change 1.
7 Swim	To move through water using one's body parts. Change 1.
8 Swig	A small drink of a liquid. Change 1.
9 Swing	To move back and forth. Add 1.
10 Wings	What the poet wishes for in the poem. Rearrange the letters.

Allan Wolf

Something about Allan Wolf

Hello Po-Folk!

My name is Allan Wolf, proud member of the species *Poemo sapiens* (but I just use the common term *Po-Folk* for short). That means that I am a human who sees the world through a poet's eyes! Every one of us humans is born a member of species *Poemo sapiens*. Being a Po-Folk means that you listen and you pay attention and you observe. I started being a Po-Folk about a month after I was born when I first noticed my own arm. At first, I thought someone had snuck it into my crib overnight. But then I realized that it was actually a part of me.

And that's the first lesson of being a Po-Folk: **Po-Folk see the world as if seeing it for the very first time**. When I was in fourth grade, I wrote my first "book." It was about an alien who lived on a crunchy salad crouton orbiting Earth. Later, as a 12-year-old, when I was feeling sad and lonely, I instinctually began to write about it on my bedroom walls. I realized, in that moment, that writing was a way to help me make sense of all the feelings bouncing around inside my head and my heart. My parents were super cool, and gave me total permission. So, I wrote on those walls for the next 47 years!

And that's the second lesson of being a Po-Folk: **Po-Folk write it down!** I don't recommend you go home and start writing on *your* bedroom walls. A nice notebook or journal will do, somewhere to write down what you do from day to day. Simple.

I am very bouncy. When I sit down to write, I have to wear noise-cancelling headphones to help myself concentrate. And I take a break every 45 minutes or so, to juggle or play guitar. Then I'll sit down again. I've been noticing things and writing them down now for 60 years. I like to research things that interest me and then turn the facts I learn into poems. That's how I learn stuff. And that's how I write books. I find one topic I like and then write a bunch of poems around that one topic, and voila! – I've written another poetry book!

I've written a whole lot of books. Here are just two that you may like. The first one is the collection that the poem "Greenhouse

Guesses" is from. It's all about a school garden. The second one is a collection of poems about the solar system! How cool is that? Happy reading Po-Folk. And metaphors be with you!

Two of Allan's books that he recommends to you:

> *Behold Our Magical Garden: Poems Fresh from a School Garden* by Allan Wolf. Illustrations by Daniel Duncan (Candlewick Press, 2022).
>
> *The Day the Universe Exploded My Head: Poems to Take You into Space and Back Again.* Illustrations by Anna Raff (Candlewick Press, 2019).

Allan Wolf, a member of the species *Poemo sapiens*, lives in Western North Carolina, where the Blue Ridge Mountains hold hands with the Smokey Mountains. He is the author of a whole lot of poetry collections, picture books, and young adult novels that combine his love of research and poetry. He is also a performance poet who shares his poetry in schools and libraries. Most importantly, Wolf believes in the healing powers of poetry writing and recitation, and he has memorized nearly a thousand poems. *Booklist* magazine says, "Allan Wolf makes reading and writing poetry cool." His motto for life: Metaphors be with you! To find out more about Allan Wolf, go to www.allanwolf.com or just google him.

A Poem by Allan Wolf

The poem I've chosen for you to experience is called "Greenhouse Guesses." The title is a "play on words" because it sounds like Greenhouse Gasses, which are the harmful fumes that get trapped in our planet's atmosphere and weaken Earth's protective ozone layer. Planting new plants is a great way to help combat the bad effects of greenhouse gasses. In this poem I wanted to show how even young people like yourself are capable of having big dreams and ambitions.

GREENHOUSE GUESSES

Five little sprouts in a greenhouse tray.
Dreaming of the plants they'll become one day.

The first little sprout, with a whimsical chant,
says, "Maybe I'm a sun-gold tomato plant!"

The second little sprout says, "Oh, my gosh!
Maybe I'm zucchini or an acorn squash."

The third little sprout says, "Maybe I'm a pea,
Or a bean, or a carrot, or a broccoli."

The fourth little sprout thinks long and hard.
"Maybe I'm a spinach. Or a lettuce. Or a chard."

The fifth little sprout says, "What will *I* be?
Maybe I'm the world's tallest redwood tree
with an eagle's nest at the very tip-top,
and leaves of gold, and an ice cream shop!"

The moral is: No matter how small they seem,
even little sprouts can dream big dreams.

From *Behold Our Magical Garden: Poems Fresh from a School Garden* by Allan Wolf. Illustrated by Daniel Duncan (Candlewick Press, 2022).

A Word Ladder by Timothy Rasinski

In a word ladder game, lead students from one word to the next by adding, subtracting, or changing one or a few letters from the previous word. Start at the top and work toward the bottom.

1 House	A structure in which people live.
2 Hose	A flexible tube of rubber or plastic through which a liquid can pass. Take away 1.
3 Rose	A flower that grows on a plant or vine that has thorns. Change 1.
4 Rise	To stand after lying, kneeling, or sitting. Change 1.
5 Risk	A chance of getting hurt or losing something. Change 1.
6 Rink	A smooth surface of ice used for ice skating or ice hockey. Change 1.
7 Rind	The thick outer layer or covering of oranges, lemons, and melons. Change 1.
8 Grind	To crush or make by crushing into very small pieces or a powder. Add 1.
9 Grin	A smile. Take away 1 letter.
10 Green	Combine with #1 to make a structure for growing plants. Replace vowel with 2.

Amy Ludwig VanDerwater

Something about Amy Ludwig VanDerwater

Hello Poetry Friends,

    I write to you with a few things by my side: my old leather notebook, my poppy mug filled with chocolate and rosebud tea, a crackling fire on this chilly Western New York morning, and our silky black cat Fiona who is lounging happily by this fire. There is a bit of frost on the grass outside, and this morning I wrote in my notebook, brought in some firewood, knitted on a rainbow hat, and listened to a story about the Salem witch trials. It has been a busy time filled with small, good things. See, I do not own a television or watch video games because I fear losing time to them, and I do work to protect my brain from the pull of my cell phone. Having hobbies and seasonal chores helps with this, and writing each morning usually points the ship of my brain and heart in a good direction. Our three cuddly kitties help with this too!

    As a young girl in Vestal, NY, I loved many of the same things I love now, especially making crafts and baking. I would create little houses for my stuffed animals and crazy big Halloween costumes out of dishwasher boxes. My friends and I stamped down forts in fields and built rock forts by the side of a creek. Once I tried to get us all to dig our own inground pool, and even though we didn't complete it, the dreaming was fun. I adored picking strawberries then and still do. These days, I make jars and jars of jam from the berries we pick each summer, last year more than 100 jars. Remember this – the things you love now can be with you forever. Feast your mind and heart on beauty and curiosity now, and it will stay with you.

    In college, I studied English and also Education at the State University of New York at Geneseo and received my master's degree at Teachers College, Columbia University in Curriculum and Teaching. I have been lucky enough to be a fourth-grade teacher, a fifth-grade teacher, and mostly a writing teacher who travels all around working with wonderful teachers and students like you. I also teach from my blog, "The Poem Farm," which is the internet home I built in 2010, posting a poem each and every day for a year and, from then on, each Friday. Every April, I post a daily poem around a certain theme, and I am always surprised by what turns up on the page.

Truth be told, my favorite part of writing is the surprise. Having published books is neat, but my favorite writing is the writing that hasn't shown up yet. When not writing or teaching in schools, I speak at conferences and teach workshops. I enjoy baking cookies and bread and learning new things about art and reading fiction, especially stories with a wee bit of magic. Our children are grown, and my husband and I cherish this old farmhouse and its land. Soon I hope to learn to be a flower gardener and maybe… to paint my flowers. Taking action and giving bring me the greatest joy. I wish you the joys that only you can find…

Peace,

Amy LV

A Poem by Amy Ludwig VanDerwater

People who make art of all kinds are inspired by other makers. Visual artists listen to music and poetry and paint works from this listening. Writers find inspiration in paintings and symphonies. Musicians take in writing and art, crafting new songs. We all learn from each other in this world, and we can discover more about what we think and feel in the works of others, even if these works were made long ago or in places far away from where we live. I wrote this poem while looking at a postcard of Vincent van Gogh's painting "Corridor in the Asylum," painted more than 135 years ago in southern France.

DOORS

Do I choose this door or do I choose that door?
The hallway of life is door upon door.
Each door has a doorknob. Each opens to secrets.
Each opens to secrets I long to explore.
One secret. One doorknob. Daily I choose
a doorway to walk through. At times I'm confused
for I know that each door is a new day to live,
a new way to struggle, a new way to give.
I stand in this hall lined with doors, doors galore
knowing each doorway will open to more,
seeking the one that will make me feel free,
turning a doorknob to find a new me.

This poem was first published on October 20, 2023 at The Poem Farm blog (www.poemfarm.amylv.com/2023/10/write-from-art.html).

Two books of mine that you might enjoy are: *With My Hands: Poems About Making Things* (Clarion, 2018) and *Write! Write! Write!* (Astra, 2020). To find all kinds of poetry book suggestions, visit the back of this book.

A Word Ladder by Timothy Rasinski

In a word ladder game, lead students from one word to the next by adding, subtracting, or changing one or a few letters from the previous word. Start at the top and work toward the bottom.

1 Door	An opening through which one enters or leaves a room or building.
2 Floor	The lowest surface in a room. Replace first letter with 2.
3 Flood	Too much rain may cause this to happen. Change 1
4 Food	What we eat. Take away 1.
5 Fog	A thick mass, like a cloud, made up of tiny water drops floating in the air near the ground. Replace 2 letters with 1.
6 Jog	To run in an easy manner. Change 1.
7 Log	A large, thick piece of a tree that has been cut down and is ready for sawing, burning, or building. Change 1.
8 Lob	To throw or toss gently. Change 1.
9 Slob	A person who is not very neat. Add 1.
10 Knob	Combine with first word to make a device to open or close doors. Change first 2 letters.

Avis Harley

Something about Avis Harley

I was born in 1941 in Vancouver, British Columbia. With my two sisters and brother, we grew up in a house in West Vancouver, surrounded by trees and a view of the sea. We had bears that would come into our back yard and eat the raspberries my mother had planted. We used to watch them from the kitchen window. Our dog would bark herself silly.

As a young child, I listened to lots of poetry and nursery rhymes recited by my mother. The rhythm and rhyme of these poems remained in my head and I think that is one reason why I began to love poetry. I always enjoyed playing with words and writing poems, and kept a daily diary (with a key).

I always wanted to be a teacher, and when I was in Grade 9, I joined The Future Teacher's Club. During my final year in high school, I had a wonderful teacher who introduced me to many poets and creative writing ideas.

I graduated from the University of British Columbia with a B.A. and a Master of Arts degree. I loved teaching at schools in Canada and England, and later gave a poetry course for teachers and librarians at the University. Giving poetry presentations in Canada, the U.S., Hong Kong, and Japan were wonderful experiences where I met people from different countries.

Music has been an important part of my life. I enjoy playing my ukulele and taking piano lessons once a week. For years I sang with the Vancouver Opera Chorus. Such fun to sing in a costume on stage with an orchestra, conductor, and his baton!

In 1970, my husband and I bought a house in Vancouver, and it is where our son grew up. I still live here and love the old house. It will be 100 years old in 2025. It's aging, just like me!

My favourite quote about writing poems is by Robert Frost:

"Poetry begins in delight and ends in wisdom."

A Poem by Avis Harley

HONEY BEE QUIZ

How many honey bees could live in one hive?
    Fifty thousand crowded together, and they thrive.

How fast do wings go back and forth in flight?
    Twelve thousand beats a minute: a buzzy delight!

How many eggs does a Queen Honey Bee lay?
    One thousand up to two thousand, day after day.

How many nectar-juicy flowers does a bee sip?
    Fifty to a hundred blossoms by the end of her trip.

How much honey will a Nectar-Collector get?
    About a twelfth of a teaspoon for a lifetime of sweat.

How many stomachs has each honey bee got?
    Two. One to store nectar and the other to eat a lot.

How many eye does every honey bee need?
    Five! Colors and shapes are the words they read.

    Though bee be wee where would we be
     if we should neglect their guarantee
      to pollinate every plant and tree?
      We are very grateful to the bee:
       this solo Keeper-of-the-Key
        of a Honey Gold recipe.
        Where would we be
         without these
         life-giving
          Bees
           ?

Here are two books you might like to read. I have written and illustrated *The Monarch's Progress: Poems with Wings* and also *Sea Stars: Saltwater Poems,* with photographs by Margaret Butschler. Both of these poems are in Wordsong books and published by Boyds Mills Press.

A Word Ladder by Timothy Rasinski

In a word ladder game, lead students from one word to the next by adding, subtracting, or changing one or a few letters from the previous word. Start at the top and work toward the bottom.

1 Bees	A flying insect that makes honey.
2 Beet	An edible plant with a red root. Change 1 letter.
3 Meet	To come face to face with another. Change 1.
4 Melt	Ice will do this when the temperature rises above 32 degrees. Change 1.
5 Milk	A white liquid produced by cows or female goats and collected for people to drink. Change 2 letters.
6 Mink	A small mammal whose dark brown and soft fur is considered very valuable. Change 1.
7 Monk	A man who is a member of a religious community and has taken a vow to live a simple life. Change 1.
8 Monkey	A small mammal that is one of the primates. Add 2.
9 Money	The coins or paper notes of a country used to buy things or pay for services. Take away 1.
10 Honey	What bees like to make. Change 1.

Betsy Franco

Something about Betsy Franco

When I was growing up in Shaker Heights, Ohio, I wanted to be an artist. I was always happiest when I was drawing or painting. I also wrote stories and drew pictures for them. In college, I majored in art, and I kept painting at night, even while I was working as a teacher. But once I had three sons, I didn't have time to set up my paints. I knew I had to be creative, so I switched to writing. Boom. It worked! After many years of writing fun books for teachers, I was able to *just* write my own books. I love to show how math and science can be funny, sassy, and creative, especially in poetry.

To get ideas for my poems, I walk to an elementary school every morning – I'm the constantly visiting author. I'm also inspired by my three creative sons and my grandson. To make a living writing books takes a lot of work and stubbornness and belief in myself. And don't forget luck. It's a lot of fun, too. I wake up every morning feeling happy about my job.

Hey, if you want to be a writer or an artist or a musician or anything creative like that, you can, too! It may take a lot of work, stubbornness, and luck… but go for it! Someone gets to do it. Why not you?

I'm lucky to be an award-winning author of over 80 books. I write children's poetry and picture books, novels, screenplays, and graphic novels. I am particularly known for my fun books that combine poetry with math and science. I was a studio art major at Stanford, and received my Master's in Education from Lesley College/Shady Hill School. I'm honored to have received a number of awards including Bank Street Best Books of the Year, Parenting Magazine Book Pick, NCTE Notable Poetry Book, Junior Library Guild Selection, and the Mathical Book Prize Award, among others. I also enjoy acting on TV and film, consulting on the film sets of my screenplays, and mentoring young people who want to be artists of some kind.

A Poem by Betsy Franco

EXCAVATING THE LOST AND FOUND

We graphed the stuff in Lost and Found
  before they hauled it away.
We spent almost half an hour
  sorting and counting that day.

We lined the water bottles up,
  tossed sweatshirts into a pile.
(I found my favorite hoodie there —
  it was missing for a while.)

We counted jackets, shoes, and toys
  and one cool cowboy hat.
The strangest?
  The pajama top.
We couldn't make sense of that!

From *Counting in Dog Years and Other Sassy Math Poems* (Candlewick Press, 2022).

Two book titles:

Counting in Dog Years and Other Sassy Math Poems by Betsy Franco. Candlewick Press, 2022.
Bees, Snails, and Peacock Tails by Betsy Franco. Margaret K. McElderry Books, 2008.

A Word Ladder by Timothy Rasinski

In a word ladder game, lead students from one word to the next by adding, subtracting, or changing one or a few letters from the previous word. Start at the top and work toward the bottom.

1 Found	Past tense of the word "find."
2 Fond	Having loving or kind feelings toward another. Take away 1.
3 Pond	A small lake. Change 1.
4 Pod	A long, thin, firm pouch that contains the seeds of a pea or bean plant. Take away 1.
5 Pad	A piece of soft material used as cushioning for protection or comfort. Change 1.
6 Paw	The foot of an animal. Change 1,
7 Saw	A tool for cutting wood. Change 1.
8 Sow	To plant or scatter seeds over the ground. Also, an adult female pig. Change 1.
9 Slow	Not fast. Add 1.
10 Slot	A narrow notch or opening into which something may be put. Change 1.
11 Lost	Opposite of found. Rearrange the letters.

Charles Ghigna

Something about Charles Ghigna

My name is Charles Ghigna. Most kids call me "Father Goose." I have the best job in the world. I write books for children!

I live in a hundred-year-old cottage in the storybook world of Homewood, Alabama. I have lived here for the past 50 years. My writing room is in the attic. I call it my "tree house." Each day after breakfast, I climb the narrow steps up to my tree house where I sit looking out over the treetops to the sky. I daydream and imagine new worlds to write about. Sometimes those daydreams turn into poems. Sometimes they turn into books!

I've written more than 5,000 poems and 100 books. One of my newest books is *The Father Goose Treasury of Poetry*. It contains 101 of my favorite poems for children. Another one of my new books is a picture book based on the true story of my great grandfather who came from Italy to make his life in America as a bookbinder. That book is *Bound to Dream: An Immigrant Story*.

During my school assembly programs, I talk about how books are little magic carpets that take us places we've never been, places real and imaginary. My magic carpet books have taken me all over the world from Alabama to Alaska, from Florida to Texas, from New York to California, from cities across England and France to South America and beyond. It will be exciting to discover where your books will take you.

People ask me where I get my ideas and what I like to write about. My ideas come from everywhere because I like to write about everything! I write about Nature, art, animals, children, pets, sports, family, friends, and the real and imaginary people and visions I "see" during my daily hikes. My wife is a poet. We like to inspire each other with new ideas. Our son is an artist. His paintings often inspire us too.

I know you are going to be inspired by this book of poems and by the stories of each poet's life. I hope this book will inspire you to write poems of your own, and to tell the stories of your life. I began keeping a journal when I was your age. Some of those journal entries turned into stories and poems. I had no idea then that my early writing habits would lead me into this wonderful world of writing. I was recently asked what's the best part of being a writer. I said: "The greatest reward for a children's author is in knowing that our efforts might stir the minds and hearts of young readers with a vision and wonder of the world and themselves that may be new to them or reveal something already familiar in new and enlightening ways."

May your future readings bring you many magic carpets, and may your writings be full of wonder and joy for yourself and others.

A Poem by Charles Ghigna

YOU ARE A POEM

Your walk is your rhythm.
Your talk is your rhyme.
Your heartbeat, your meter
That keeps perfect time.

Your name is your title.
Your mind, inspiration.
You are a poem—
A precious creation!

This poem was first published in the March 2024 issue of *Highlights for Children*.

Here are two other books of mine you might enjoy. *The Father Goose Treasury of Poetry* (Schiffer Kids, 2023) and *Strange Unusual Gross & Cool Animals* (Simon & Schuster, 2023).

A Word Ladder by Timothy Rasinski

In a word ladder game, lead students from one word to the next by adding, subtracting, or changing one or a few letters from the previous word. Start at the top and work toward the bottom.

1 Title	The name of a book, poem, or song.
2 Tile	A flat piece of baked clay or other hard material and used to cover floors, walls, or roofs. Take away 1 letter.
3 Mile	A distance of 5,280 feet. Change 1.
4 Lime	A small green citrus fruit. Rearrange the letters.
5 Lame	Having difficulty walking or running. Change 1.
6 Male	Another name for a man or boy. Rearrange the letters.
7 Tale	Another name for a story. Change 1.
8 Tame	Not wild. Change 1.
9 Same	Being alike in every way; not at all different. Change 1.
10 Name	What the poet says is the title of your poem. Change 1.

Charles Waters

Something about Charles Waters

Hey there! When I was your age, I was so obsessed with sports that few things mattered more. I watched them on TV, attended a handful of games, and read anything I could get my hands on that was sports related in newspapers. Any kind of book which didn't include sports didn't interest me. This is why the poem I have for you in this book is a sports one. Looking back on it, I wasn't as curious about the world as I am now.

My hope for you is to develop a sense of curiosity about the world and not wait until you're an adult to admire such wonders as witnessing the star patterns decorating the sky, admiring ribbons of colors stretching across a sunrise or sunset, and hearing the melodious chirping of birds singing their songs.

Curiosity will help you become a more well-rounded individual. It's fine and dandy to be focused on something; however, make sure to pay attention to the world around you as well. There's so much to see and experience, and that, my friends, is where many potential poems are waiting for you.

Charles Waters is a children's poet, actor, and author who has co-created various books with Irene Latham including *Can I Touch Your Hair? Poems of Race, Mistakes and Friendship*, which was named an NCTE Charlotte Huck Honor; *Dictionary for a Better World: Poems, Quotes and Anecdotes from A to Z*; *African Town*, winner of the Scott O'Dell Award for Historical Fiction, and *Be a Bridge*. His book *Mascot* (co-written with Traci Sorell) has won multiple awards including an American Indian Youth Literature Honor.

A Poem by Charles Waters

MOMENT IN THE SUN (or A BACK-UPS BACK-UP)

Since football season started
I've done nothing but ride the pine.
For one shining second –
I'd love a moment that's *mine*.

It happened when my teammate
got hurt and couldn't play,
Coach Smith yelled "You're in McGirt,
stay out of everyone's way."

"Green 19, ready, set, hut!"
A blur came before my eyes
I stood there in a state of shock
when all of a sudden … SURPRISE!

I sacked the star quarterback
for a 22-yard loss,
It felt like I was smothered
in a vat of awesome sauce.

Coach gave me the game ball
"How did you do that, Jake?"
I shrugged my shoulders then said,
"It was a piece of cake."

A Word Ladder by Timothy Rasinski

In a word ladder game, lead students from one word to the next by adding, subtracting, or changing one or a few letters from the previous word. Start at the top and work toward the bottom.

1 Piece	A section or part separated from the whole.
2 Pie	A dessert served at the end of a meal. Take away 2.
3 Pine	What the poet rode in most football games. Another name for the bench. Add 1
4 Spine	Another name for our backbone. Add 1.
5 Shine	What lights do. Change 1.
6 Line	A long, thin, straight mark. Replace first 2 with 1.
7 Like	To enjoy or find pleasure in someone or something. Change 1.
8 Lake	A body of fresh water. Change 1.
9 Rake	A garden tool used to gather leaves, sticks, and other yard debris. Change 1.
10 Cake	Combine with first word to refer to something easy to do.

David L. Harrison

Something about David L. Harrison

Hi kids. Can you look at my picture and imagine me as a third grader? I was one... 78 years ago. I attended Oak Grove Elementary School in Springfield, Missouri. My favorite subjects were math, spelling, and art. During recess I loved playing softball. Basketball? Not as much. Oak Grove was a rural school so many of my friends lived on farms. For their 4-H projects they got to do fun things like raise calves or pigs. We lived in a little old rented house with no place to raise animals so for my project I started an insect collection.

After a while my collection expanded to include other items of interest found in fields, flower gardens, and along roadsides where I went prowling with my butterfly net. My bedroom became a slightly smelly den adorned by abandoned turtle shells, wings off dead birds, snake skins, animal skulls, and whatever else caught my eye. By seventh grade, when my pet parakeet died (his name was Tim), I cried and buried it. Next day I dug it up and added its wings and skull to my collection. Okay that's weird, but I feel sure you would do the same thing.

When I went to college, I chose to become a biologist. I think it all started with my 4-H hobby in third grade. After graduating from Drury College (university now) in Springfield, I went to Emory University in Atlanta, Georgia to earn a Master's degree. Guess what I studied there? Parasites. Please don't say "oh yuck." Parasites are important! The one I studied was a little guy found mostly in rats. I raised my own rats in the laboratory. Did I just hear another "yuck?" Where are your manners??

So here we are, meeting in a book. I can't think of a better place to meet. I started writing books for young people more than 50 years ago. I help write books for teachers, too, for them to use in their classrooms. I write for seven hours each weekday and I have learned four things. One, I love to write. Two, I love to write for kids. Three, I love to write poems. And four, I remember being in third grade.

Here's something called a bio. It's mostly a list of things I've done and some nice results that have happened along the way.

David L. Harrison has served as poet laureate for the state of Missouri (2023–2025) and for Drury University. He has received dozens of awards for his 110 books for children and teachers, including Society of Midland Authors Award for Best Children's Nonfiction Book; Christopher Medal for fiction; Texas Bluebonnet Award Master Reading List; National Science Teachers Association list of Outstanding Science Trade Books; and Master List of Finalists for the State of Kansas Bill Martin, Jr. Picture Book Award. He received the 2023 Celebrate Literacy Award from Missouri Literacy Association. His work has been widely translated and anthologized more than 200 times. David is a regular presenter at conferences, workshops, literature festivals, schools, and colleges. He holds a Bachelor of Arts degree from Drury University, a Master's degree in Science from Emory University, and two honorary doctorates of letters. David Harrison Elementary School is named for him.

A Poem by David L. Harrison

We all have good days but now and then we have one that's not so hot. Things just seem to go wrong. I wrote this poem for everyone on the entire planet who has had a bad day.

MONDAY

Overslept
Rain is pouring
Missed the bus
Dad is roaring

Late for school
Forgot my spelling
Soaking wet
Clothes are smelling

Dropped my books
Got them muddy
Flunked a test
Didn't study

Teacher says
I must do better
Lost my money
Tore my sweater

Feeling dumber
Feeling glummer
Monday sure can be
A bummer.

This poem was in a Wordsong book published by Boyds Mills Press in 1993 and called *Somebody Catch My Homework*.

Here are two other books of mine that you might like to read. *The Dirt Book: Poems About Animals that Live Beneath Our Feet* (Holiday House, 2021) and *Wild Brunch: Poems About How Animals Eat* (Charlesbridge, 2024). At the end of this book, you'll find a long list of titles by the poets in *40 Poems for 40 Weeks* plus many others.

A Word Ladder by Timothy Rasinski

In a word ladder game, lead students from one word to the next by adding, subtracting, or changing one or a few letters from the previous word. Start at the top and work toward the bottom.

1 Bummer	A word that describes something as bad or poor.
2 Bumper	A metal or plastic piece on the front and back of cars and trucks that protects the car from damage if it hits something. Change 1.
3 Bump	To knock against something. Take away 2.
4 Stump	What's left of a tree after it is cut down. Replace first letter with 2.
5 Lump	A small mass or pile with no special shape. Replace first 2 letters with 1.
6 Lamp	A device that gives off light. Change 1.
7 Damp	Slightly wet. Change 1.
8 Dam	A wall built across a river or stream to keep the water from flowing and to raise the water level behind it. Take away 1.
9 Day	24 hours. Change 1.
10 Monday	The day of the week that is a bummer for the poet. Add 3.

Eileen Spinelli

Something about Eileen Spinelli

I fell in love with poetry when I was five years old. It was a summer Saturday afternoon. My mother took me to the public library. We walked. It felt far and adventurous. The children's section was on the second floor. I climbed the steps and into a wonderland. Books everywhere! Books about bears and bees and bunnies. Books about trees and trucks and triangles. Books with pictures. Books with poems. I didn't know which book to grab first. It made no difference to me that I couldn't read. The librarian suggested Robert Lewis Stevenson's book *A Child's Garden of Verses*.

That night my mother read the poem "Bed in Summer." It begins:

> In winter I get up at night.
> And dress by yellow candle-light.
> In summer quite the other way.
> I have to go to bed by day.

That year I visited the library every Saturday with my mother. The following year I was allowed to go with my older friend, Gladys. By then I had learned to read. And I learned something else: what I wanted most of all was to become a writer. Specifically, a poet.

My father gave me his old manual typewriter. The Z key stuck. Fine. I would not write about zebras or zippers. He made me a desk from a wooden orange crate. My mother filled a box with paper. And that's how I began. Two-fingered typing. Letters into words. Words into poems. In high school I won a poetry contest. With the prize money I bought myself a better typewriter. I also bought myself a pair of red high heels. I won a dance contest wearing those shoes – but it was writing poems, not dancing, that stole my heart.

Many years later a *someone* stole my heart. My husband and fellow author, Jerry Spinelli. Jerry and I try to write most mornings. After breakfast we each head to our separate offices.

My office looks out onto a small wood and past the woods to a lake. There is a lot of wildlife outside my window. Deer, red foxes, raccoons, squirrels, and turtles. There are many birds including crows and hummingbirds; bluebirds and cardinals; noisy geese and sometimes a blue heron. And although this wildlife can distract me from my work, I consider those distractions happy and productive ones.

I write longhand first – in my comfy writing chair, which is yellow with a pattern of roses. Then I type what I've written into the computer. Jerry and I meet before lunch – either in his office or mine – to share what we've written that morning. We give each other honest feedback. And always – encouragement.

The rest of the day is given over to daily life: errands, household chores, cooking, reading, taking walks, meals, movies, thrift shopping, hanging out with family and friends. Some days we go to a play at a local theater. Some nights we sit out with cups of tea and listen for owls. Some nights we read poems aloud. I still love the poem "Bed in Summer."

A Book Bio: Once I passed the 50 mark on published books I stopped counting those and started counting grandkids. So I don't know the exact number of books I've published. But they include picture books such as: *Thanksgiving at the Tappletons*; *Miss Fox's Class Goes Green*; *When You are Happy*; *The Best Story*; and *Somebody Loves You, Mr. Hatch*. My novels-in-verse include: *Another Day as Emily*; *The Dancing Pancake*; *Summerhouse Time*; and *Birdie*. *Somebody Loves You, Mr. Hatch* was rejected by 24 publishers before the twenty-fifth said yes. The book has gone on to win several awards including the Christopher Award. It has been turned into a puppet presentation as well as a film by Axis Theatre Company in Canada. A good lesson in perseverance.

A Poem by Eileen Spinelli

A POEM CAN

A poem can begin
with anything–
an empty swing in winter
a noisy crow
waving goodbye to your best friend
or maybe hello.
A poem can start with
turtles…or mud…
or a scary thud in a dream.
It can start with an orange moon
or a blue balloon sailing
across the sky.
But no matter how a poem begins,
all the best ones end
with the same thing:
a sweet, unexpected ripple
in your heart.

Two books I recommend:

Stargirl by Jerry Spinelli. Ember; Reprint edition, 2002.
The Poetry Friday Anthology compiled by Sylvia Vardell and Janet Wong. Pomelo Books, 2012.

A Word Ladder by Timothy Rasinski

In a word ladder game, lead students from one word to the next by adding, subtracting, or changing one or a few letters from the previous word. Start at the top and work toward the bottom.

1 End	A point in time at which something stops or finishes.
2 Den	The lair or home of a wild, usually predatory, animal. Rearrange the letters.
3 Hen	An adult female chicken. Change 1.
4 Pen	An instrument used for writing with ink. Change 1.
5 Pan	A kitchen utensil used for frying food. Change 1.
6 Tan	To make brown by exposure to the sun or to a special lamp. Change 1.
7 Tar	A dark heavy substance used to cover roads. Change 1.
8 Tart	A small baked pastry shell with a fruit or other filling. Add 1.
9 Art	The creation of things whose purpose is to be beautiful or full of meaning. Take away 1.
10 Heart	Where poems produce an unexpected ripple. Add 2.

Ellen Hopkins

Something about Ellen Hopkins

Did you know there are entire books in verse? Like, long stories written totally in poetry, complete with characters, dialogue, and plots with dramatic twists, or that make you laugh. Maybe you've read one like *Starfish* by Lisa Fipps or *Love That Dog* by Sharon Creech. I highly recommend both. But guess what? I write them, too.

Most of my novels-in-verse are young adult, for older teens. But I also have two you can read now, with more on the way. You'll find their titles below. Funny thing. When I first started writing fiction, only a few other authors took a chance on crafting novels this way. Most editors didn't want them because they didn't understand the power of poetry as storytelling. But readers did and do!

They love the musical quality, almost like lyrics on the page. They love the white space that allows them to pause and consider the careful placement of every well-chosen word. They love the sounds, patterns, and flow, and how they don't get mired in big blocks of text. Now, lots of authors publish verse novels, and I take pride in knowing I helped pave the way.

My own journey began long, long ago, in a faraway place called Palm Springs, California. My mom adored books, read to my brother and me every day, and had me reading chapter books before kindergarten. I've always been a huge reader, and my writing sprang from that. Sprang. Cool word. Anyway, poetry has always been my preferred form, and I published my first poem at nine years old. Just about your age. I bet you could, too!

I studied journalism in college and was a freelance journalist for many years. During that time, I was raising a family, and started thinking about writing for young people, too. Some of my articles seemed like good subjects, and the first 20 books for kids I published were nonfiction. Not in verse.

But I was still writing poetry, and my poem here is a reimagined version of a picture book I wrote. It won the Society of Children's Book Writers and Illustrators Sue Alexander Award, and I got to show it to a Simon & Schuster editor. She loved it, but didn't work on picture books, and asked if I had something for older readers. That led to me publishing my first young adult (YA) novel-in-verse, *Crank*. Yes, this poem jumpstarted my successful 20-year-old fiction career.

Bio: Ellen Hopkins is the award-winning author of 20 nonfiction books for children, four novels for adult readers, two middle-grade novels-in-verse, and 14 NY Times bestselling young adult verse novels. Her fifteenth YA novel was published in August 2024, and she's currently working on her third middle grade novel, *Finding Olivia*. Her books have won numerous state awards, and one was nominated for the National Book Award. Ellen is a Nevada Hall of Fame award winner, and her name hangs on a University of Nevada, Reno wall beneath Mark Twain's. After six decades in the West, she moved with her extended family and two brilliant German Shepherds to a log home on five wooded Missouri acres.

Recommended for you: *Closer to Nowhere* (Nancy Paulsen Books, 2020) and *What About Will* (Nancy Paulsen Books, 2023), both by Ellen Hopkins.

A Poem by Ellen Hopkins

NIGHT WORLD

Outside my window
when day dims to night and shadows
stretch deep into fading light,
a strange new world awakens.

The sky glitters gold
as one by one, stars flicker
on, sun upon sun, inviting
dark's creatures to roam.

When doves fold their wings
in evening prayer, billows
of bats take to the air
like thunderclouds on the hunt.

Tarantulas march, daddy long
legs prance, the garden jumps
with the eight-legged dance,
sticky webs bob between leaves.

Over the fence, in meadow
grass deep, jack rabbits hurry,
gopher snakes creep,
whiskers twitch and eyes glow green.

Through the pine curtain
deep in the grove, owl leaves
his perch, bear starts to rove,
hungry bird and beast on the prowl.

Lunar eyes peek over the hill,
watch raiding raccoons
as coyotes trill, silhouettes
captured in moonbeams.

'Neath the rusting gate, silver
mouse runs bold, fragrant skunk
plods home, sunrise fog crawls cold,
moles and marmots find burrows.

As eastern knolls color
with lavender light and yellow
moon pales to ghostly white,
night world settles into slumber.

A Word Ladder by Timothy Rasinski

In a word ladder game, lead students from one word to the next by adding, subtracting, or changing one or a few letters from the previous word. Start at the top and work toward the bottom.

1 Shadows	Dark images cast on a surface by a person or thing blocking the light of the sun or another source of light.
2 Show	To demonstrate something to others. Take away 3.
3 Shoe	A protective covering for the foot, usually made of canvas or leather. Change 1.
4 Hoe	A garden tool used for breaking up soil and removing weeds. Take away 1.
5 Hot	Opposite of cold. Change 1.
6 Shot	Past tense of "shoot." Add 1.
7 Knot	A tying together of material such as rope, string, or yarn in order to fasten. Change first 2 letters.
8 Knit	To join together loops of yarn by hand with long needles or by machine, in order to make items such as sweaters and blankets. Change 1.
9 Knight	A soldier on horseback in the Middle Ages. Add 2.
10 Night	Combine with first word to indicate what the poet says the day dims into. Take away 1.

Eric Ode

Something about Eric Ode

Hi, friends.

Have you had a favorite writing assignment in school?

When I was in second grade, our teacher, Mrs. Beach, asked us to write a story as if we were jack-o-lanterns. We were supposed to share what we saw and what we thought about as we sat there on a front porch on a chilly October evening. In my story, I included a line about someone sticking a candle inside me, and it was giving me heartburn. I remember Mrs. Beach reading my story out loud to the class. The kids laughed. They loved that line.

That felt really good, writing something that made other people happy. Maybe more importantly, that line made *me* happy. When I came up with that idea – of a jack-o-lantern with heartburn – it surprised me.

That is the earliest memory I have of discovering that, with words, we can craft new, maybe surprising ideas – ideas that surprise even ourselves!

I can remember writing a few poems in school. But I didn't really get serious about writing poetry until I was teaching. I mostly taught fourth grade. We used a lot of poetry in my classroom – all forms and styles of poetry by any number of different poets. I fell in love with the language and the surprising ideas crafted by Valerie Worth. We also dove into the poetry of Robert Frost, of course, and Eileen Spinelli and Shel Silverstein and Ogden Nash and Judith Viorst… So many amazing poets! So many surprising ideas!

Being surrounded by all of that amazing poetry made me want to try my own hand at writing poems. I wanted to see if I could come anywhere near to writing the kinds of poems I was discovering and enjoying.

Now, when I'm in the schools, it's as a visiting author and poet and songwriter. What a privilege! Over and over again, when I'm leading writing workshops, the students surprise me with new ideas – ideas I never would have considered on my own.

My favorite poems tend to be the ones that surprise me – that make me look at something in a new way. I hope this poem, "OSCAR CAN'T JUMP," gives you something new to think about. It's a true poem. Well, maybe every poem is true in its own way. But this poem is true through and through.

A Poem by Eric Ode

OSCAR CAN'T JUMP

Oscar can't jump.
It's not that he's too old.
His bones grew wrong.
And so, he's never told
to shoo
from where he does not belong
the way you do
when you have a cat
who can jump.

You never wake
to find him
sitting on your face
when you were only hoping
to take
a quick nap.
He never bats
the violets
from the windowsill
the way some cats will.

And, when you are wrapped
in a good book,
he's not crowding your lap,
keeping you
from turning the pages.
That is unless
you reach down,
lift him up,
and set him there.
Which you
will almost certainly do
because you will remember
Oscar can't jump.

Two books of mine you might enjoy include *Stop That Poem!* (illustrated by Jieting Chen) and *Otters, Snails, and Tadpole Tails: Poems from the Wetlands* (illustrated by Ruth Harper). Both are from Kane Miller Books.

A Word Ladder by Timothy Rasinski

In a word ladder game, lead students from one word to the next by adding, subtracting, or changing one or a few letters from the previous word. Start at the top and work toward the bottom.

1 Oscar	The name of the character in the poem.
2 Car	Another name for an automobile. Take away 2.
3 Can	A cylindrical container for holding and preserving food. Change 1.
4 Cant	Unable to do something. Add 1 – Be sure to add an apostrophe.
5 Rant	To scold or complain vehemently. Change 1.
6 Runt	An animal that is unusually small for its age. Change 1.
7 Run	To walk at a fast pace. Take away 1.
8 Pun	The humorous use of a word in such a way as to suggest two or more of its meanings. Change 1.
9 Pup	A young dog. Change 1.
10 Pump	A mechanism for drawing oil or water out of the ground. Add 1.
11 Jump	What Oscar cannot do in the poem. Change 1.

Georgia Heard

Something about Georgia Heard

Hi there, young poets and readers! I'm Georgia Heard, and I'm all about writing from the heart. When I was your age, I carried around a special notebook where I wrote down all my thoughts and feelings. It was like my own secret treasure chest of words!

As I grew older, I discovered a new way to spread joy through words – I started writing birthday poems for my friends and family. It was amazing to see how a few carefully chosen words could light up someone's day like a candle on a birthday cake.

Now, I live in sunny South Florida with my family, surrounded by nature and the ocean. You might find me strolling along the beach, searching for seashells and watching for baby sea turtles crawling out of their nests into the sea.

But before I settled in Florida, I went to a special place called poetry school (yes, there is such a thing!) at Columbia University in New York City. There, I studied the art of poetry and earned my MFA, which stands for Master of Fine Arts, in poetry. The city was like a playground for my imagination, full of people, buses, taxis, and rain puddles that mirrored the sky.

I've had the privilege of writing more than 20 books, and I'm incredibly grateful to have been honored with the 2023 NCTE Award for Excellence in Poetry for Children. This award recognizes the body of work of a living American poet, and I feel fortunate to have received it.

Teaching writing is another passion of mine. I've spent years helping kids and grown-ups alike explore the power of words. One of my favorite books I've written is my new edition *Awakening the Heart: Teaching Poetry in Elementary and Middle School*, where I share all the wonderful things I've learned about poetry.

If you're eager to learn more about me, check out my website at www.georgiaheard.com or find me on Twitter/X and Instagram @georgiaheard1.

A Poem by Georgia Heard

I've always been fascinated by the way snakes shed their skin. Did you know you can actually pick up their shed skin and take a closer look? That's why I wrote this poem, to celebrate the wonder of snakes and how when they shed their skin it's kind of like the way humans change their clothes.

DRESSING LIKE A SNAKE

A snake changes its clothes
only twice a year.
Beginning with its nose,
peeling down to its toes:
new clothes suddenly appear.
Would it be nice
to dress only twice
instead of each day of the year?

This poem was published in a book called *Creatures of Earth, Sea and Sky* by Boyds Mills Press.

Here are two other books of mine you might like to read: *Welcome to the Wonder House* (Wordsong, Astra Books for Young Readers, 2023) co-written with my friend and fellow poet, Rebecca Kai Dotlich and *My Thoughts Are Clouds: Poems for Mindfulness* (Roaring Brook Press, 2021).

A Word Ladder by Timothy Rasinski

In a word ladder game, lead students from one word to the next by adding, subtracting, or changing one or a few letters from the previous word. Start at the top and work toward the bottom.

1 Nose	A part of the body on the face.
2 Hose	A flexible tube of rubber or plastic through which a liquid can pass. Change 1.
3 Host	A person who entertains guests. Change 1.
4 Cost	The price of something. Change 1.
5 Cast	In fishing, to throw the rod and line out into the air. Change 1.
6 Past	Opposite of future. Change 1.
7 Post	A pole or stake placed upright in the ground to mark or support something. Change 1.
8 Pots	Several kitchen utensils used for cooking. Rearrange letters.
9 Dots	Little marks or spots. Change 1.
10 Does	More than one young deer. Change 1.
11 Toes	A snake changes its clothes from its nose to this point. Change 1.

Greg Pincus

Something about Greg Pincus

When I was a young boy, even younger than you are today I suspect, I started writing poems in every birthday card I made for my family. I still haven't stopped writing poems, even though now I suspect I'm much older than you are today. Maybe it's in my blood – the doctors tell me my blood type is ABAB – but whatever the reason, it's undeniably true that I love poetry.

In high school, I had poems published in the school literary magazine and wrote a hugely epic piece of poetry as my major English class project... which is why it surprised a lot of people when I went to college to study computer science. But computers had been another passion of mine ever since I first got to program one (that filled up a whole room), and in some ways I found that writing good programs and writing good poetry shared a lot in common. In the end, I got a degree in creative writing as well as one in computer science and immediately moved to Hollywood to try and write movies. Because... well... I loved poetry and computer science, for sure, and I really loved the movies, too.

Eventually, I mixed in my love of baseball with storytelling and wrote a movie called *Little Big League* that you can still watch today. Later on, I wrote a few movies for the Disney Channel and everything from 10-minute cartoons to two-hour long TV movies. I've also written a couple novels for kids, and I've kept on writing poetry, too, lots of which has been published in books and magazines, on the Internet, and, most importantly of all, in family birthday cards.

A Poem by Greg Pincus

My parents really did try to teach me to save money. It is a very good skill to have, but I didn't always think it meant the same thing that they did…

HOW I SAVE MONEY

My parents always tell me "Saving money is the key."
Now, I've figured out a lot of ways that saving works for me.

Today, in fact, I saved a dollar eight from being sad –
I used it for some candy, and I know that made it glad.

Last week, I saw some quarters in a fountain at the mall…
So, I saved them all from drowning (and they bought a basketball).

My allowance funds get lonely, but I save them if I spend 'em,
And I get them into registers where lots of bucks befriend 'em.

And just the other day I bought… well… I don't know what you call it,
But I saved two twenty-dollar bills from rotting in dad's wallet.

I know a lot of other tricks, but I don't want to bore you.
Instead, just send me all your cash. I'll gladly save it for you!

    I think you might enjoy my novels *The 14 Fibs of Gregory K.* and *The Homework Strike* (both from Arthur A. Levine Books/Scholastic). The books are about a boy named Gregory who doesn't like math, truly hates homework, and really loves poetry and pie.

A Word Ladder by Timothy Rasinski

In a word ladder game, lead students from one word to the next by adding, subtracting, or changing one or a few letters from the previous word. Start at the top and work toward the bottom.

1 Save	To rescue from harm or danger. Also, to keep and accumulate for future use.
2 Sale	The selling of goods for a lower price than usual. Change 1.
3 Tale	Another name for a story. Change 1.
4 Male	A person who is a boy or man. Change 1.
5 Mole	A small, permanent spot on the skin that is usually brown and sometimes slightly raised. Also, a small mammal with small eyes that lives underground. Change 1.
6 Hole	An opening in something. Change 1.
7 Home	A structure in which a person or family lives. Change 1.
8 Hone	To sharpen or improve a skill or talent. Change 1.
9 Honey	A food produced by bees. Add 1.
10 Money	What the poet is supposed to save in the poem. Change 1.

Heidi E.Y. Stemple

Something about Heidi E.Y. Stemple

When I was a kid, I didn't want to be a writer when I grew up. I did write a lot – especially about nature. I was raised by a writer mom and a birdwatching dad. My brothers and I would create our own field guides, sometimes with realistic birds and animals, and sometimes with fantastical creatures. We wrote poems that my mom copied so we could have "books" of our poetry. But I had other ideas for a grown-up job. So, when I went to college, I studied social work, psychology, and criminal justice. After I graduated I became a probation officer in Florida, then a private investigator (which sounds more exciting than it actually is). It wasn't until I was 28 years old that I gave in and joined the family business, publishing my first short story in a book called *Famous Writers and Their Kids Write Spooky Stories*. The famous writer was my mom, author Jane Yolen. We followed that up quickly with our first book together, *Meet the Monsters* (illustrated by Patricia Ludlow) that we finished revising just two weeks before my daughter was born. I thought writing would be a hobby while I had a baby at home, but, as it turns out, writing is something I am not only good at, but I also really love it.

Now, my thirty-seventh book just landed on bookshelves. I have 11 more under contract, and I write poems, and short stories, and books for all ages. I also teach writing to writers just starting out. When asked to write this poem, I had just finished reading a book in which all the kids loved to write but really disliked math. So, I thought I would write an opposite poem – all about the thrill of math.

I live on a big old farm in Massachusetts with a dozen deer, a family of bears, three coyotes, two bobcats, a gray fox, a red fox, tons of birds, an enormous racoon, and some very fat groundhogs. Once a year, I wake up at midnight and head out into the wood with a team of birders (we call ourselves the OMG, which stands for the Owl Moon Gang). All night, we call and count owls for the Audubon Christmas Bird Count, the longest-running citizen science project in the world. You can read about the Bird Count in my book *Counting Birds* illustrated by Clover

Robin. My newest (2024) books are *Wren's Nest* illustrated by Eugenia Nobati, *She Sells Sea Shells* illustrated by Emily Paik, *Dodo Dodgeball* illustrated by Eva Bryne, and *We Celebrate the Light* co-authored by Jane Yolen and illustrated by Jieting Chen. Poetry is still one of my favorite things to write – look for my novel in verse in 2025 called *The Poetry of Car Mechanics*.

You can usually find me in my book-filled office or at www.HeidiEYStemple.com.

A Poem by Heidi E.Y. Stemple

I LOVE MATH

I wake each morning
ready for school,
and at the risk
of sounding too uncool,
I put on my shoes
sequentially–
excitement growing
exponentially.
Adding, subtracting,
and, oh yes, fractions!
All give me equilateral
satisfactions.
When calculating
I can clearly see
the evens and odds,
X, Y, and Z.
Make a triangle,
measure all its parts.
I choose math
over any
language arts.
Show my work?
I am always willing.
Because math is
the square root
of everything
thrilling.

A Word Ladder by Timothy Rasinski

In a word ladder game, lead students from one word to the next by adding, subtracting, or changing one or a few letters from the previous word. Start at the top and work toward the bottom.

1 Square	A shape with four straight sides of equal length.
2 Squire	A young nobleman who served as a knight's attendant. Change 1.
3 Acquire	To get or obtain. Replace first letter with 2.
4 Cure	Something that makes a sick person healthy or well. Take away 3 letters.
5 Cute	Another word for pretty. Change 1.
6 Cut	To slice or open with a sharp tool such as a knife, ax, saw, or scissors. Take away 1.
7 Cot	A portable bed used in camping. Change 1.
8 Hot	Very warm. Change 1.
9 Rot	To decompose or decay. Change 1.
10 Root	Combine with first word to make a mathematical operation. Add 1.

Irene Latham

Something about Irene Latham

Hello from Alabama!

I wasn't born in Alabama, but I have lived here most of my life – it's where I went to high school and college, where I got married, and where my husband and I raised our three sons. And now it's the place where I write stories and poems.

But that's not all I do.

I fill the feeders and watch the hummingbirds buzz in. I tend a small container garden, coaxing fresh tomatoes and basil from seed to table. I paint and read and play cello in my Purple Horse Poetry Studio & Music Room. I walk with my husband and our Australian Shepherd Rosie every morning along our quiet country road. We boat and fish and kayak and take lots of photos of the sky and water and wildlife. One year we watched a pair of bald eagles collide in mid-air, then descend in the slow swirl of feathers that's known as the eagle mating spiral. Another time we watched a herd of at least 20 deer emerge from the morning fog then disappear again.

Each day there's something beautiful to experience and write about. And each day I think about you out there, somewhere.

You, who are a young reader and dreamer, just like I once was – and still am in my heart. I think about all the things you and I have in common: how we both get mad sometimes and are happy other times; how we eat and sleep and dream; how we have questions, curiosities, and wonders.

Mostly I think about how I can use words to connect us across decades and distance. I wonder about what you're doing, and I imagine how we might meet in a book or a poem. You are the person I'm thinking of when I choose topics and fuss over words and rearrange lines in poems.

I want to show you the world the way it looks to me. I want to tell you my story. And I want to hear your story, too.

For now, I want you to know that I started writing when I was very young. My first pieces were love poems – for my mother. I'm still writing love poems! In fact, you can read a fresh poem from me each Friday at my website www.irenelatham.com as part of my (free!) ArtSpeak series, which features poems inspired by art. My college degrees are in social work, and I didn't take a single writing course in college. I'm most proud of the Mouster's degree I earned as a participant in the Walt Disney College Program. Because I'm a shy person by nature, it took me a long time to get brave enough to try to find publishers for my poems and stories. Now I'm the author or co-author of more than 20 books for children, some of which have won awards like a Caldecott Honor; a Charlotte Huck Honor; the Scott O'Dell Award for Historical Fiction; and others. I was once named Poet of the Year by Alabama State Poetry Society and Most Promising Poet for Children by the International Literacy Association. For many years I was a visiting author at schools around the country. But the best reward of all is hearing from readers. I love mail! If you write me a letter or email, I promise to reply: irene@irenelatham.com or PO Box 122, Oneonta, AL 35121.

Meanwhile, I invite you to check out *This Poem is a Nest* (WordSong, 2020), one of the most joyful books I've ever written and possibly the one that feels the most "me." Also, be sure to check out an anthology of poems I co-curated with my Poetic Forever Friend Charles Waters. It's called *The Mistakes That Made Us: Confessions from Twenty Poets* (Lerner, 2024). Happy reading!

A Poem by Irene Latham

The poem I've chosen to share with you is one I'd hoped would appear in my collection *Fresh Delicious: Poems from the Farmer's Market* (WordSong, 2016). That book is filled with love poems to and about some of my favorite fruits and vegetables. But this particular poem didn't make the cut.

When you read it, I hope you see not just me – and strawberries! – but yourself, too.

STRAWBERRY SELF-PORTRAIT

Juicy, sweet, delectable:
That's me.

But do you see?
I'm also bumpy, grumpy.

My skin is pink in places
it ought not be.

My cap is crooked
and ants have chewed

a hunk out of me. See?
My brothers are bigger,

my sisters sweeter.
But it's fine, it's okay.

I'm the only me
there will ever be.

A Word Ladder by Timothy Rasinski

In a word ladder game, lead students from one word to the next by adding, subtracting, or changing one or a few letters from the previous word. Start at the top and work toward the bottom.

1 Portrait	A drawing or painting of a person.
2 Trait	A characteristic or quality that makes a person or animal different from others. Take away 3.
3 Train	A connected series of railroad cars. Change 1.
4 Grain	The small hard seeds of cereal plants such as wheat or rice. Change 1.
5 Grin	Another name for a smile. Take away 1.
6 Grill	The rack of metal bars used to hold foods for cooking over flames. Replace last letter with 2.
7 Spill	To cause or allow to flow or fall from a container. Change first 2.
8 Spell	A word or group of words used to make magic. Change 1.
9 Sell	To exchange with another person for money. Take away 1.
10 Self	A word that refers to you. Combine with first word to make the type of portrait the poet wants to make. Change 1.

Jane Yolen

Something about Jane Yolen

Hi, Kids,

It's not so much that I always wanted to be a writer; I simply thought all grown-ups were published book writers. My parents' friends all wrote books. Their friends included writers like James Thurber and Ernest Hemingway, and newspaper reporters, and sports writers, who brought many of their latest books as gifts for my parents when they came for dinner, and there they all talked and talked and talked about writing.

My dad was head of the Overseas Press Club for 20 years, My mother wrote short stories and made up and sold crossword puzzles and double-crostics.

And while I knew there were teachers and butchers, and cab drivers and doctors and nurses and subway conductors (we lived in New York City), I thought that after that daily work, they each went home to write.

Well, maybe it's truer than it sounds. After all, I became first an editor and then a writer. My brother Steve became first a musician and then a well-known newspaper writer and foreign correspondent.

And here I am now, author of close to 500 published books. Lots of short stories, poems, song lyrics, a couple of opera librettos (that's the words part of opera) on the boil, some movies… Yes – as an adult I became a published writer, just like my parents and all their grown-up friends.

And now my three children and two of my grandchildren have books out. My daughter's new book coming out soon is called *Janie Writes*. And yes, it's about me writing a play and a musical for first grade. It was all about vegetables. I played the chief carrot in our performance. We ended up singing a song I wrote called "Vegetable Salad and Soup."

So you might become a published author, too. Even if you are a doctor, a lawyer, a nurse, a teacher, or president of the United States first.

Your book friend,
Jane Yolen

A Poem by Jane Yolen

ANTELOPE DEFINED

He's not a running insect.
He's not C-minus fruit.
He looks a bit just like a deer,
In fact, he's pretty cute.

In case you haven't heard, he's not
A bison, goat, or sheep,
So counting him is hard to do
When you go off to sleep

But should you go to Africa,
You'll find him by the dozens,
Along with almost 90 of
His closest loping cousins.

A Word Ladder by Timothy Rasinski

In a word ladder game, lead students from one word to the next by adding, subtracting, or changing one or a few letters from the previous word. Start at the top and work toward the bottom.

1 Antelope	An animal with horns, a long neck, long legs, and hooves.
2 Lope	An easy, usually bounding, gait or running style capable of being sustained for a long time. Take away 4.
3 Pole	Either end of a planet's, moon's, or star's axis. Rearrange the letters.
4 Pale	Light in color. Change 1.
5 Pace	The rate at which one walks. Change 1.
6 Space	The area that contains the entire universe beyond the Earth. Add 1.
7 Spice	A substance with a unique smell or taste and used to flavor food and drink. Change 1.
8 Mice	More than one mouse. Replace first 2 letters with 1.
9 Rice	A food grain usually grown in warm, wet areas of the world such as parts of India, China, and Japan. Change 1.
10 Africa	Add 2 letters to the beginning and change the last letter to make the continent on which antelopes are found.

Janet Wong

Something about Janet Wong

When I look at this picture, I remember feeling very happy that day, despite the fact that we were living through a pandemic. I felt happy because our son, who is grown up and lives far away from me and my husband, was visiting home that week. He took this picture of me while I was getting ready to do a Zoom visit with a school, which is another reason why I was happy. I love working with students. While it was difficult to travel during the pandemic, it was very easy to connect with kids all over the world. On one day in Spring 2020, I started my day at 7 o'clock by zooming with students in Spain (Madrid), then met students in the United States (New York and Seattle), followed by students in China (Shanghai). I ended that long day by sharing poems with students in Thailand (Bangkok). At midnight I was tired from all my talking, but I felt so energized that it took me a long time to fall asleep.

Something that you might already know about me, especially if you've read my "Meet the Author" book *Before It Wriggles Away* (Richard C. Owen Books, 2006), is that I used to be a lawyer. In my last law job, I was Director of Labor Relations at Universal Studios Hollywood. Some lawyers make the world a better place, but I didn't feel that I was doing important work. I wanted to make a difference, and I couldn't think of anything that was more important than working with kids. "I should become an elementary teacher," I told myself. But I knew I could not be a teacher. When I was working my way through Yale Law School, one of my jobs was being a substitute teacher, and being a teacher is the hardest job I've ever had. So why did I become a children's author? While looking for a gift in a children's bookstore, the idea hit me: somebody wrote these books. And books make people think. They inspire readers to do good things, to be kind and fair, and to feel happy. I figured that if I wrote children's books, I could make a difference in this world with my words – and I could also work with kids once in a while as a visiting author. I quit my law job and took a chance on my dream. After more than a year of rejection letters, I sold my first book. Thirty years later, I now have created more than 40 books and have visited thousands of schools, where I've met tons of kids: smart, funny, thoughtful readers and writers just like you.

Here is a bio statement that highlights some of the "big things" in my life:

Janet Wong is a graduate of Yale Law School and a former lawyer. She has written more than 40 books for children on a wide variety of subjects, including chess (*Alex and the Wednesday Chess Club*) and her Asian heritage (*Good Luck Gold & MORE*). She is the 2021 winner of the NCTE Excellence in Poetry for Children Award, a lifetime achievement award that is one of the highest honors a children's poet can receive. When Janet is not working, she is often playing pickleball. Learn more about Janet at janetwong.com.

A Poem by Janet Wong

At some schools, students say the pledge of allegiance at the start of the day. If you don't say it – or if you love the rhythm of the pledge and want to experiment with putting your own words into it – here's my poem "Let's Pledge Between Us" to inspire you.

LET'S PLEDGE BETWEEN US

Let's pledge between us:
to be kind

and remind ourselves
every morning
to be respectful
and honest and true,

each person
looking out
for the other,

doing what's right,
acting responsibly
in fairness
for all.

This poem first appeared in a book called *Great Morning! Poems for School Leaders to Read Aloud* by Sylvia Vardell and me (Janet Wong). This book is an anthology of 75 poems by more than 50 poets, including many of the poets in this book. School principals like sharing this book during morning announcements. They often invite student leaders to be guest readers using this book.

I usually create anthologies with my friend Sylvia Vardell that include poems by dozens of poets, but I'm especially proud of two books of mine where I wrote all the words. One is *Twist: Yoga Poems*, illustrated by Julie Paschkis (McElderry/

Simon & Schuster, 2007), which will make you want to stand up and stretch. I wrote that book as a gift for the illustrator Julie Paschkis because she loves to do yoga every day. *Knock on Wood: Poems about Superstitions* (McElderry/Simon & Schuster, 2003) is another book written by me and illustrated by Julie Paschkis. Look for that book if you ever feel like you need more luck!

A Word Ladder by Timothy Rasinski

In a word ladder game, lead students from one word to the next by adding, subtracting, or changing one or a few letters from the previous word. Start at the top and work toward the bottom.

1 Be	To live or exist.
2 Bet	To agree to pay if one's guess about some future event is wrong. Add 1 letter.
3 Jet	An engine for an airplane that gives off a backward flow of heated gases to cause forward movement. Change 1.
4 Pet	A domestic animal such as a dog or cat that lives with a person or family. Change 1.
5 Pit	A hole in the ground; also the hard seed at the center of a cherry, plum, or other fruits. Change 1.
6 Pint	A measure of volume – 16 ounces. Add 1.
7 Ping	To emit or make a short, sharp, high-pitched sound, as of metal striking metal. Change 1.
8 Wing	A body part that allows birds and some insects to fly. Change 1.
9 King	The male head of a royal family. Change 1.
10 Kind	What the poet asks us to pledge – to be _____ Change 1.

Joseph Bruchac

Something about Joseph Bruchac

Kwai Nidoba – those words mean "Hello friend" in Abenaki, a Native American language some of my ancestors spoke. I also can greet you by saying Ahoj Kamarat in Slovak, from my father's side of the family. That means "Hello friend" too.

You may have guessed by few things about me. One is that I like to start any conversation in a friendly way. You never can tell when you're going to make a new friend. Another thing is that I am proud of all my ancestors. (I'll bet some of you are like me and have more than one ancestry.) And the third thing is that I love words.

I have always loved reading and writing ever since I can remember. By the time I was in second grade, I was memorizing poems and trying to write poems of my own. I loved second grade and my second-grade teacher, Mrs. Monthany. She encouraged me to write.

Now I have to confess something to you. I did not love third grade. I was an unhappy third grader. That was because I was sent to a different school. Saratoga, Springs, where I went to grade school, had a lot of elementary schools. School Number One, Number Two, Number Three, Number Four, and so on. I spent kindergarten, first and second grades in School Two. But then, for some reason, I was sent to School Three for third grade. I did not know anyone. The building was not familiar to me. Bigger kids bullied me and I don't remember anything I liked about that school year. Maybe some of you are having a hard time now in third grade. Sometimes, for all kinds of reasons, school can be tough. But it is important not to give up. There is always the chance that things can get better and every day brings a new sunrise.

What helped me to get through third grade was doing things like walking in the woods and spending time with my grandparents who always listened to me and encouraged me.

I survived third grade and next year I was sent back to my beloved School Two for fourth grade and my teacher Miss McTygue was the best teacher I ever had. One day, she and her sister came to my house and brought me a maple sapling. We planted that tree together in my backyard. Today it is taller than my house.

I have always loved the natural world and written a lot about it. When I went to college at Cornell University, I studied wildlife conservation and majored in English. The first time I had a poem published was in a student magazine at Cornell. That was over 60 years ago. I have had hundreds of poems published since then and many books.

And I now have grandchildren of my own, who also love words and writing poetry. Just as my grandparents did with me, I listen to them and encourage them.

Here are a few things that might help you get to know me a little better. I've written a lot of books of all kinds for all ages – more than 180 of them now. (You can read about them on my website joebruchac.com.) Some are books of poetry, some are novels, some are nonfiction, and some are poetry picture books illustrated by wonderful artists like my old friend Thomas Locker. I'd like to recommend two of my books of poetry that he illustrated so you can see what I mean. *Thirteen Moons of Turtle's Back* (that I co-wrote with Jonathan London) (Puffin Books; Reprint edition, 1997) and *The Earth Under Sky Bear's Feet* (Puffin Books; Illustrated edition, 1998).

Now here's a little about me aside from my writing. I have two grown sons, James and Jesse. They both write books for kids and have kids of their own – my three grandchildren Carol, Jacob, and Ava. My sons Jim and Jesse and I all have black belts. We teach martial arts together at our own dojo. Together we run the Ndakinna Education Center (ndakinnacenter.org). We teach about Indigenous culture and language and the natural world – on our 90 acre nature preserve.

In addition to my Bachelor of Arts degree from Cornell and my Master's degree from Syracuse University, I also have a Ph.D. from the Union Institute. But I think I learned more from two places other than college. The first was West Africa, where I was a volunteer teacher in Ghana for three years. That taught me so much about other cultures and ways of seeing the world. The second was from prisons, where I did poetry workshops for many years. That experience taught me that poetry can make lives better. People who've made big mistakes can change.

Two more little facts about me. My wife, Nicola Marae Allain, is from the island of Tahiti. Sometimes we go there to visit her relatives. The two of us are licensed wildlife rehabilitators. We care for hurt and orphaned wild animals until they are ready to be released.

A Poem by Joseph Bruchac

WHEN YOU PLANT A TREE

When you plant a tree,
the way my teacher
did with me,
you are holding hands
with the future.

You are reaching out
to those you know
and also those
whose faces you
may never see.

You are giving
to the world
a place where birds
may build their nests
and creatures of all kinds
may come to stay.

And if one day
that tree bears fruit
you may not be
the one to pick it,
but others will
appreciate the gift
that you gave.

A Word Ladder by Timothy Rasinski

In a word ladder game, lead students from one word to the next by adding, subtracting, or changing one or a few letters from the previous word. Start at the top and work toward the bottom.

1 Tree	A woody plant that lives for years and has a usually single tall main stem.
2 Tee	A peg on which a golf ball is placed before being struck. Take away 1.
3 Toe	One of these is found at the end of your feet. Change 1.
4 Doe	A female deer. Change 1.
5 Done	When a job is complete we say it is _____. Add 1.
6 Dine	To eat or to take dinner. Change 1.
7 Line	A narrow elongated mark drawn between two points. Change 1.
8 Life	The time period from birth to death. Change 1.
9 Lift	To raise up. Change 1.
10 Gift	What the poet describes trees as. Change 1.

Joyce Sidman

Something about Joyce Sidman

I grew up in Connecticut, the middle sister of three. Although we each had our own interests, we sisters played together and got into trouble together. I distinctly remember us venturing into a wetland near our home (despite being strictly forbidden to do so) and coming home with frogs and salamanders and sneakers full of mud.

I loved being outside. I loved my friends. I loved writing and drawing and reading and singing and play-acting. I loved school and most of my teachers, although I sometimes talked too much and got sent out into the hall. I loved candy, and would carefully plan clandestine bike rides to the drugstore to buy it.

Words and phrases came into my head, and I wrote them down (this began in elementary school). Later, I kept journals. I felt compelled to write. I think a lot of writers are like this; writing helps us understand the world. I also really needed (and still do) "pondering time." Time alone, without noise and distraction. For me, this is when ideas come – not just for writing, but for life. My pondering time usually happens during walks in the woods. The natural world sustains and inspires me.

I love poetry because it is vivid and sleek, like a race car – no extra words. I've always been drawn to its images and metaphor; they are such a powerful way of explaining your thoughts and feelings (as in poetry = race car). I kept writing poetry all through school and into adulthood. After the birth of my two sons, I decided I wanted to write poetry for children. I feel incredibly lucky to be doing what I always dreamed of: creating books.

Here are some standard biography facts: Joyce Sidman is the author of many award-winning children's poetry books, including the Newbery Honor-winning *Dark Emperor and Other Poems of the Night*, and two Caldecott Honor books. Her book *The Girl Who Drew Butterflies: How Maria Merian's Art Changed Science* won the 2019 Robert F. Sibert Medal for Nonfiction. Joyce also has received the NCTE Award for Excellence in Children's Poetry for her body of work. In her home state of Minnesota, she teaches poetry writing to school children and walks through the woods with her dog Watson.

A Poem by Joyce Sidman

I love to write about animals, and do lots of research to find out what their lives are like. This poem is about California deer mouse babies, whose father helps keep them warm in their snug nest until they grow fur. It's from my book *Just Us Two: Poems About Animal Dads* (Millbrook Press, 2000).

MOUSE HAIKU

Blind and tissue-skinned,
tiny mice enter the world
in a nest of grass.

Hide-and-seek masters,
they will soon whisk, surefooted,
through the chill spring night.

Until then, Father
warms this fragile thimbleful
of fluttering hearts.

If you like reading about animals, you might enjoy my books *Dear Treefrog* (Houghton Mifflin Harcourt, 2021) and *Winter Bees and Other Poems of the Cold* (Houghton Mifflin Harcourt, 2014).

A Word Ladder by Timothy Rasinski

In a word ladder game, lead students from one word to the next by adding, subtracting, or changing one or a few letters from the previous word. Start at the top and work toward the bottom.

1 Hide	To put something out of sight.
2 Chide	To nag or goad by criticizing. Add 1.
3 Chime	A bell, or the sound of a bell. Change 1.
4 Chick	A baby chicken. Change last 2 letters.
5 Lick	What you do with a lollipop. Replace first 2 letters with 1.
6 Pick	To choose. Change 1.
7 Peck	What chickens do with their beaks to pick up things. Change 1.
8 Peek	To look quickly or secretly. Change 1.
9 Meek	Timid; not easily upset. Change 1.
10 Seek	To look for something. Combine with first word to make the name of a game. Change 1.

Kalli Dakos

Something about Kalli Dakos

Poetry has helped me to find strength, resilience, and courage in this world. The great words of poetry are like good friends that travel with me and inspire me to take risks, to accept failure, and to do my best.

I grew up in Canada, but moved to the United States when I was an adult. I lived in Nevada, New York and Virginia before I moved back to Canada many years later. I love both the land where I was born and my adopted land.

I became a teacher and then a reading specialist, but I always knew I wanted to be a writer too. One year, I decided to take time away from teaching and to work on my writing. I have been writing ever since.

When I returned to the classroom, I found the *best stories of all* right inside my own school. It was as if I went back to teaching wearing a pair of "magic glasses" and they were letting me see all the stories in my school. These stories seemed to fit best in poetry, and I wrote poems with funny titles like:

If You're Not Here, Please Raise Your Hand
A Funeral in the Bathroom
The Bug in the Teacher's Coffee

I have written over 3,000 poems about the school world and I keep finding more to write about – bookbags, pencils, the Lost and Found, desks, friendships, teachers, recess, lunch, bugs in the classroom, and so much more!

The poems have been published in my many books of poetry, and my book *They Only See the Outside* won an Award for Excellence in Poetry from the NCTE. Several of my books have been Children's Choice Selections, and I am so happy that the students chose these books as favorites.

I had a fascinating experience on a playground in the far north of Canada, and it inspired the poem that I will share with you today. I taught in a school that is 60 miles above the Arctic Circle in a town called Inuvik.

During several of the winter months, in the far north, it is dark all day and it is dark all night. The children go to school in the dark, they have lunch in the dark, they have recess in the dark, and they go home in the dark.

I was on the playground at recess during the dark season when the northern lights danced across the sky in such beauty that we felt as if we were dancing with them. We couldn't move away from all this beauty, even when the bell rang for us to go back inside.

A poem was inspired that day by these amazing lights, and it is the poem that I would like to share with you.

I learned an important lesson as a writer. The most amazing stories of all are not in books or in the movies or on television. They are stories we live every single day of our lives with each other. I hope you will put on those "magic glasses" and look for the stories and the poems. There is so much to celebrate in this world!

A Poem by Kalli Dakos

THE NORTHERN LIGHTS

The northern lights
put on a show
in the polar sky.
They pranced,
they danced,
kept us entranced,
a whirlwind up high.

The colors streamed
in blues and greens
with rosy red rays.
They lit the night
with wild light
across the Milky Way.

We couldn't run.
We couldn't play.
We couldn't even speak.
In a daze,
we just gazed
till our legs went weak.

Faraway
we heard the bell,
to call us back inside.
We didn't move.
We were glued,

to the wonders in the sky!

This poem was published by DC Canada Education Publishing and is in my book *Recess in the Dark, Poems from the Far North*. Here are two other books of mine that you might like to read – *They Only See the Outside* (Magination Press, 2021) and *Our Principal Promised to Kiss a Pig* (Albert Whitman, 2004).

A Word Ladder by Timothy Rasinski

In a word ladder game, lead students from one word to the next by adding, subtracting, or changing one or a few letters from the previous word. Start at the top and work toward the bottom.

1 Wonders	Things or events that cause amazement.
2 Won	Past tense of win. "We ___ yesterday's game." Take away 4.
3 Son	Opposite of daughter. Change 1.
4 Song	A short musical composition for singing. Add 1.
5 Sing	What you do with a song. Change 1.
6 Spring	The season after winter. Add 2.
7 Spin	To turn around rapidly. Take away 2.
8 Skin	The tissue or covering for our bodies. Change 1.
9 Ski	To move over snow on a pair of long, narrow, smooth runners. Take away 1.
10 Sky	Where you find the wonders in the poem. Change 1.

Karen Craigo

Something about Karen Craigo

I've always enjoyed playing with words and stories and sounds. I think it might date back to that very first childish experimentation with language. I grew up on Dr. Seuss, and that playful approach to language made a big impression on me. You wouldn't call anything I wrote "poetry" until the second day of my first poetry workshop in college. The first day, I turned in a truly godawful poem about rainbows, and my soon-to-be mentor, the late Michelle Boisseau, read it and very quickly had me giggling about how over-the-top it was. I turned in something much better for my second class, and I've been trying to top myself with every attempt since.

If you ask me my preference for how I write, I'll tell you that I like to work in the mornings with a long legal pad and a particular blue pen. I write poems in one long sitting, typically, and I revise on my computer so I can see how things would line up on the printed page. But my process has always been to destabilize myself and not to be too dependent upon factors like that. If I start to think I can write only in the morning, I give myself the challenge of writing before bed or in the afternoon at a coffee shop. I replace the legal pad with a notebook, a scratch pad, the back of an envelope; I replace the pen with a pencil or keyboard. The thing is, writing time is a little limited for most of us who try to make art while also working and being a parent. I can't be a princess about it. I'm always sort of in training to use my time as it becomes available with whatever tools are at hand.

My kids are both sages. They say the most intriguing things, and they inspire me all the time. Heck, some of my poems can be directly traced back to Facebook posts where I quote their quirky remarks. I don't know what I'll do when they're out of the house! Guess I'll have to go back to making things up...

My husband, Michael Czyzniejewski, is a brilliant fiction writer (www.overdrive.com/media/2155768/i-will-love-you-for-the-rest-of-my-life) – moving and hilarious! I don't know why they don't have a fiction laureate. He'd be my choice. He's certainly the laureate of my heart.

A Poem by Karen Craigo

NEW YEAR

This morning, the first
of a new year, new decade,
I fell down the stairs—
the whole flight, feet first,
then sideways, with a rump—
pump-pump at the bottom.
I sat there a minute, touched
all my parts, flexed my arms
and legs, and it turns out
I'm fine, not a scratch
or bump, so take that,
year: Bring me your worst,
and I will give it back to you,
unscraped, astounded.

A Word Ladder by Timothy Rasinski

In a word ladder game, lead students from one word to the next by adding, subtracting, or changing one or a few letters from the previous word. Start at the top and work toward the bottom.

1 Fell	Past tense of "fall."
2 Felt	Past tense of "feel." Change 1.
3 Melt	What ice will do when it gets warm. Change 1
4 Pelt	The skin or hide of an animal. Change 1.
5 Pet	A domestic animal that lives with people. Take away 1.
6 Pat	The shortened form of the name Patrick or Patricia. Change 1 (capitalize).
7 Part	A portion of something. Add 1.
8 Tart	A sour taste. Also a small baked pastry shell with a fruit or other filling. Change 1.
9 Start	Another word for "begin." Add 1.
10 Stars	Celestial objects in the sky that can be seen at night. Change 1.
11 Stairs	Add 1 letter to make what the poet fell down.

Kate Coombs

Something about Kate Coombs

I'm a lifelong bookworm, which is the best way to learn to be an author. When my brother and sister and I were young, our parents read three or four books to us every night at bedtime. Once when I was about three, my dad decided to conduct a little experiment on me. How long would I listen to him read stories before I got tired of it? Well, his voice ran out before I did!

Later I learned to read to myself. My sister and I rode our bikes to the library every Saturday and checked out ten books. We read them very quickly and wished they would let us check out more!

As a bookworm, I found that sometimes my parents and teachers interrupted my reading to get me to do things like eat or sleep or do homework or chores. Bookworms have to find ways of dealing with these people! There's the "read your book under the edge of your desk at school" technique, the "hide out in the backyard reading when you're supposed to be vacuuming" tactic, and the "read under the covers with a flashlight instead of sleeping" approach. That last one was a problem because my little sister told on me. So I figured out I could take my book to the bathroom late at night and read for hours. I cleverly guessed that my sleeping parents might hear me get up and go to the bathroom, but they wouldn't notice if I didn't come back.

In between reading, I babysat my little brother and sister, learned to play the oboe, took art classes, went camping, and began to write. I wrote little plays with parts like the Glorious Queen for me and the Quiet Servant Girl for my sister. During my Nancy Drew reading phase, I wrote a mystery about a girl who was a lot like Nancy. I started writing poetry, too.

In college I studied English – which is about books! I used to study in the college library right next to the children's bookshelves so I could take breaks to read those books. They were way more fun than my college classwork. I began writing short stories, almost always fantasy and fairytales. Of course, I kept writing poetry.

After college I ended up being an editor and then a teacher. I taught kindergarten through third grade in downtown Los Angeles. I had learned Spanish, which was good because most of my students' families spoke Spanish. Later I worked as a home teacher, driving around L.A. teaching seriously ill students. These days I teach college writing classes and tutor kids who are struggling readers. I live in Utah, where the snow still seems surprising to me every year and deer hang out in our backyard.

As a children's book author, I have written picture books, funny middle grade (MG) fantasy novels, lots of board books, and four poetry collections. My first poetry collection, *Water Sings Blue,* is about the ocean and its creatures. I am very pleased that it won the Lee Bennett Hopkins Poetry Award. I have had poems published in several anthologies like this one, too. I am still a bookworm, but I am also an author, and both things make me happy!

A Poem by Kate Coombs

Did you know that honeybees do a special dance to tell the other bees where to find good flowers? I wrote this poem about bees I pictured dancing in the 1950s, when a "hop" was a dance party and "bebop" was a kind of jazz music. Keep in mind that almost all bees are female.

THE HONEYBEE HOP

Let's fly down to the Honeybee Hop, girls,

Hmm, hum, hmmm!

We'll have nectar with gold on top, now

Hmm, hum, hmmm!

Everybody dressed in her pollen socks,

wings a-flutter cause we're gonna rock, yeah

Hmm, hum, hmmm!

Do a little dance with the hive jukebox,

telling 'bout the daisies and the hollyhocks, say

Hmm, hum, hmmm!

Come on, everybody, to the Honeybee Hop

cause we're all dolled up for the big bee-bop, it's

Hmm, hum, hmmm!

Hmm, hum, hmmm!

If you want to read more of my poems, try my newest book, *Today I Am a River* (Sounds True, 2023), and another fun poetry book, *Monster School* (Chronicle, 2018).

A Word Ladder by Timothy Rasinski

In a word ladder game, lead students from one word to the next by adding, subtracting, or changing one or a few letters from the previous word. Start at the top and work toward the bottom.

1 Honeybee	An insect with wings that lives in a hive and produces honey.
2 Honey	The food produced by honeybees. Take away 3.
3 Hey	A word used to draw attention or show surprise. Take away 2.
4 Hay	Grass, clover, or alfalfa that is cut, dried, and stored for animal food. Change 1.
5 Bay	A part of a sea or lake that cuts into a coastline and is partly surrounded by land. Change 1.
6 Boy	A young male. Change 1.
7 Joy	Happiness. Change 1.
8 Toy	A plaything, usually for children. Change 1.
9 Top	Opposite of bottom. Change 1.
10 Hop	A dance done by the honeybees in the poem. Change 1

Kenn Nesbitt

Something about Kenn Nesbitt

When they told me I had a whole page to tell you about myself, my first thought was, "Wait, what? How am I going to fill an entire page!?" I mean, bios are usually only a few sentences long, maybe a paragraph, not a whole page.

Then I remembered… I have a bunch of bios I wrote for different books and I realized they might fill an entire page if I just put them together. But there's a catch… only one of them is true; the rest are completely (or at least mostly) made up. Can you figure out which is the real one?

Bio 1: from *The Ultimate Top-Secret Guide to Taking Over the World*
Kenn Nesbitt was born into the noblest of families and made himself what he is today: a broken shell of a man, mumbling something about "enemies" and plotting his return to power. He was last seen hiding in a sub-basement with a ten-year supply of frozen bologna sandwiches and his no-good, backstabbing cyborg manservant, Clyde. Writing this book was the happiest four days of his life.

Bio 2: from *Revenge of the Lunch Ladies: The Hilarious Book of School Poetry*
By night, Kenn Nesbitt is a genius criminal mastermind whose work is so secret, even he doesn't know what it is. By day, he is a masked crimefighter whose sworn duty is to defeat his own diabolical plans. When not saving the world from himself, Kenn can be found writing funny poems at poetry4kids.com and visiting schools worldwide.

Bio 3: from *The Tighty-Whitey Spider: And More Wacky Animal Poems I Totally Made Up*
As a child, Kenn Nesbitt once got lost during a field trip to the zoo and was raised by animals who taught him their secret ways. He used that knowledge to create this book, every word of which is true. Really. Okay, not really. He just wanted to see if you would read the jacket flap.

Bio 4: from *A Festival for Frogs: Funny Poems for Kids*

Children's Poet Laureate (2013–2015) Kenn Nesbitt is the author of many books for children, including *The Armpit of Doom*, *More Bears!*, *The Tighty-Whitey Spider*, and *One Minute Till Bedtime*. He is also the creator of the world's most popular children's poetry website, www.poetry4kids.com.

So, did you figure it out? Of course you did. I knew you would. You're smart that way.

A Poem by Kenn Nesbitt

As a kid, I loved tongue twisters like "rubber baby buggy bumpers" and "toy boat, toy boat, toy boat." I liked the challenge of trying to say them quickly without messing up, and I loved discovering new ones.

The tongue twister I heard most often was "she sells seashells by the seashore." Sometimes people would say, "Sally sells seashells…" but I never thought that sounded right. I figured that if she's selling seashells at the seashore, her name should be something like Sandy or Shelley, rather than Sally. So, I wrote this little poem to tell her story. See if you can read it out loud without getting your tongue twisted.

SHELLEY SELLERS

Shelley Sellers sells her shells
at Shelley's Seashell Cellars.
She sells shells (and she sure sells!)
to smelly seashore dwellers.

Smelly dwellers shop the sales
at Shelley's seashell store.
Salty sailors stop their ships
for seashells by the shore.

Shelley's shop, a shabby shack,
so sandy, salty, smelly,
still sells shells despite the smells;
a swell shell shop for Shelley.

This poem appeared in my book My Hippo Has the Hiccups: And Other Poems I Totally Made Up, published in 2009 by Sourcebooks Jabberwocky.

You can find more crazy tongue twister poems in my books *The Tighty-Whitey Spider: And More Wacky Animal Poems I Totally Made Up* (Sourcebooks Jabberwocky, 2010), and *The Elephant Repairman: Funny Poems for Kids* (Purple Room Publishing, 2022).

A Word Ladder by Timothy Rasinski

In a word ladder game, lead students from one word to the next by adding, subtracting, or changing one or a few letters from the previous word. Start at the top and work toward the bottom.

1 Shack	A small, cheaply constructed building.
2 Snack	A small meal eaten between meals. Change 1.
3 Knack	A natural talent for something. Change 1.
4 Stack	To pile one on top of another. Change first 2 letters,
5 Stalk	The main stem of a plant. Change 1 letter.
6 Stall	To delay. Also, the area of a barn used to keep a single animal. Change 1.
7 Stan	A shortened form of the name Stanley. (Be sure to capitalize.) Drop 2 and add 1.
8 Scan	To read or look over quickly. Change 1.
9 Scant	Not much. Add 1.
10 Shanty	Another name for a shack or poorly constructed building. Change 1 letter and add 1 to the end.
11 Shabby	Of poor quality or worn out. How the poet describes Shelley's shack. Change 2 letters.

Laura Purdie Salas

Something about Laura Purdie Salas

Hello! My name's Laura Purdie Salas, and I'm a Minnesota author. I was actually born and raised in Florida, and I've hated hot weather since I was very young. When I was a kid, people would give me sweaters for my October birthday. I'd still be wearing shorts and flip flops to school at that point! The sweaters sat, unworn, in my dresser.

I thought I wanted to be a veterinarian when I grew up. But in eighth grade, I job shadowed our family veterinarian. While watching eye surgery on a dog, I stood very close. The combination of anesthesia the dog was exhaling and being grossed out made me feel quite sick. Maybe being a vet was not my perfect career. I considered being a wildlife biologist. I pictured myself living in a tent and studying lions and giraffes up close and personal. I was positive I'd do something with science and animals.

But then I took a creative writing class in college. I loved it, and I couldn't believe that some people made careers out of different kinds of writing. So I got my degree in English – Creative Writing from the University of Central Florida.

After that, I worked as an eighth-grade English teacher, a magazine editor, a newspaper copyeditor, and much more. I never did become a veterinarian or a wildlife biologist! My husband and I moved to Minnesota back in 1990. Our friends and family said, "You'll be back. You'll freeze in Minnesota!" But here we still are. I love having all four seasons. Just as I'm bored with one season, another one comes.

When our two daughters were little, we read with them all the time. I fell in love with picture books – which are perfect for ALL ages. I've been writing (mostly) picture books since the late 1990s. I get to explore all kinds of topics (especially science and animal subjects) and write about them. I hope my books make kids excited and curious to learn more about the things I write about.

Besides reading and writing (usually at my treadmill desk), I have many interests. I love to explore new places, play games, walk, doodle, eat too many sweet treats, knit (poorly), play kalimba (poorly), and watch competition shows on TV (competitions for baking, sewing, pottery, singing, and other things I can't do well!). I also like to talk with young writers, and I visit libraries and schools frequently (mostly virtually).

Officially, Laura Purdie Salas is the award-winning author of more than 135 poetry, nonfiction, and fiction picture books. Her titles include *Zap! Clap! Boom!*, *In the Middle of the Night: Poems from a Wide-Awake House*, *Water Can Be...*, and *Finding Family*. Some of the honors her books have earned are starred reviews, a Charlotte Zolotow Award Honor, a Riverby Award for Nature Writing, Bank Street Best Books, NCTE Notables, and the Minnesota Book Award. Visit Laura online at laurasalas.com.

A Poem by Laura Purdie Salas

I chose this poem to share because it's about the mysteries of the world and how much we still have to explore and discover. And because I love the ocean.

THE OCEAN DEEP

Far below us,
Secrets sleep.
Secrets hidden
Fathoms deep.

Much unseen.
Much unknown
Of trench and drift,
Of fin and bone,

Where creatures dwell,
Where shipwrecks go.
Let's explore
The dark below.

A Word Ladder by Timothy Rasinski

In a word ladder game, lead students from one word to the next by adding, subtracting, or changing one or a few letters from the previous word. Start at the top and work toward the bottom.

1 Shipwrecks	Damaged ships that sink.
2 Ship	A large boat. Take away 6.
3 Shape	The appearance of an object from its surface. Change 1 and add 1.
4 Shave	To remove hair from the face or body with a razor. Change 1.
5 Have	To be in possession of something. Take away 1.
6 Hate	Opposite of love. Change 1.
7 Rate	The speed or pace at which something is done. Change 1.
8 Crate	A box used for packing and shipping things. Add 1.
9 Create	To make something new. Add 1.
10 Creatures	Living things. Add 3.

Lesléa Newman

Something about Lesléa Newman

I have been writing poetry since I was eight years old, when my family moved from Brooklyn to Long Island. When we lived in Brooklyn, my grandmother's apartment was right across the street from ours; now she lived a 45-minute car ride away. I missed my grandmother terribly, and though no one told me to do this, I began writing poetry to express my feelings. This made me feel better, so I never stopped!

Writing poetry helps me understand the world outside of me, the world inside of me, and the relationship between the two. I write poetry all the time – when I'm sad, when I'm mad, even when I'm glad! There is a cellist named Pablo Casals whom I greatly admire. He once said, "My cello is my oldest friend, my dearest friend." That's how I feel about my pen. It is my oldest and dearest friend. And yes, I still write with a pen in a spiral notebook. I have been composing poems in this way for more than half a century.

Some things to know about me: I'm a big animal lover and since my parents surprised me with a puppy when I was 12 years old, I have never been without a pet. In college, I had a hamster and an iguana. After college, I was adopted by a tiger-striped cat, and I have lived with cats ever since. I write about cats a lot. And other animals. And people, too of course. Other things I love: doing crossword puzzles, going to the movies, and eating dark chocolate.

Here is a more traditional bio:

Lesléa Newman has created 86 books (and counting!) for readers of all ages.

She served as the poet laureate of Northampton, Massachusetts from 2008–2010 and initiated several projects including Poetry To Wait By (distributing poetry books to doctors' waiting rooms); Hear A Poet/There a Poet (poetry column in a local newspaper featuring local poets); and Thirty Poems in Thirty Days (a "poem-a-thon" which raised $13,000 for the Center for New Americans Literacy Project). She has received many literary awards, including poetry fellowships from the National Endowment for the Arts and the Massachusetts Artists Foundation, five Cat Writers Association Muse Medallions, two National Jewish Book Awards, the Massachusetts Book Award, the Association of Jewish Libraries Sydney Taylor Body-of-Work Award, two American Library Association Stonewall Honors, the Matthew Shepard Foundation Making a Difference Award, and the Joan F. Kaywell Books Save Lives Award. She lives in Massachusetts.

A Poem by Lesléa Newman

Though I currently live with one cat, my dream is to share my home with many, many others. Can you add up the number of cats living with the speaker of this poem?

SWEET DREAMS

Late at night when I'm in bed
With one cat perched upon my head
And two cats lying at my feet
And three cats curled beneath the sheet
And four cats dozing on the chairs
And five cats snoozing on the stairs
And six cats snoring on the floor
And seven cats dreaming by the door
And eight cats resting in a heap
And nine cats busy counting sheep
And ten cats slumbering next to me
There's no place I would rather be.

Here are two books of mine – about cats of course! – that you might enjoy: *Ketzel, the Cat Who Composed* (Candlewick Press, 2015), which is the true story of a cat who composed a short piece of music for the piano, and *Welcoming Elijah: A Passover Tale with A Tail* (Charlesbridge, 2020), which is about a cat who attends a Passover seder, and in doing so finds a new home.

A Word Ladder by Timothy Rasinski

In a word ladder game, lead students from one word to the next by adding, subtracting, or changing one or a few letters from the previous word. Start at the top and work toward the bottom.

1 Cats	Pets that belong to the feline family of animals.
2 Cast	To throw or fling, as in fishing. Rearrange the letters.
3 Past	Opposite of the future. Change 1.
4 Pest	Someone or something that annoys or bothers. Change 1.
5 Test	A set of questions to find out how much someone knows about something. Change 1.
6 Rest	To be in a state of relaxation or ease. Change 1.
7 Rent	A regular payment made to an owner of property for the right to live in or use that property. Change 1.
8 Cent	Another name for a penny. Change 1.
9 Tent	A shelter made of nylon or canvas and used when camping. Change 1.
10 Ten	The number of cats in bed with the poet. Take away 1.

Marilyn Singer

Something about Marilyn Singer

When I was a little kid, my parents read me lots of books. I especially loved fairy tales and poems. I also loved hearing my parents sing to me, which they did every night. The songs they sang were the popular hits of the day and they had great lyrics. Between the poems and the lyrics, I grew up with a real appreciation for how magical words can be.

In third grade, I started writing my own poems. At first, all of them rhymed. My teacher told me that not all poems have to rhyme and I should trying writing "free verse." So I did – and ended up with a paragraph about skating. It wasn't a poem at all!

Later on, I got better at writing poems that didn't rhyme, and still later, I started to experiment with different poetry forms. I've always liked playing word games, so fooling around with forms was kind of a game. One day when I was sitting on my couch, I looked at my cat napping across from me in a chair, and this happened:

A cat	Incomplete:
without	A chair
a chair:	without
Incomplete.	a cat.

I got excited and wondered if I could write more poems like that. So I did. A lot of them were based on the fairy tales and myths I loved. They became my three books: *Mirror Mirror*, *Follow Follow*, and *Echo Echo*, all illustrated by Josée Masse. I called the poems "reversos." A reverso has two parts. The second part reverses the order of the lines, with changes only in punctuation and capitalization, and it says something completely different from the first part.

I've now written more than 120 books in many genres, but poetry is still my favorite thing to write. I'm honored to have won the 2015 NCTE Award for Excellence in Poetry, as well as a number of other awards for my work. I still like to play games. I also love to bird-watch, garden, swing dance with my husband,

and hang out with my standard poodle, cat, and two doves in Brooklyn, NY and Washington, CT. I hope you'll try out some poetry games, too. You can let me know if you do through my website: www.marilynsinger.net.

A Poem by Marilyn Singer

LAST FLOWER

Summer
whispered good-bye.
In my garden,
the last flower
rose
a frosty white.

A frosty white
rose—
the last flower
in my garden—
whispered, "Good-bye,
summer."

A Word Ladder by Timothy Rasinski

In a word ladder game, lead students from one word to the next by adding, subtracting, or changing one or a few letters from the previous word. Start at the top and work toward the bottom.

1 Summer	The season after spring.
2 Sum	The answer to an addition problem. Take away 3.
3 Sub	Short name for a boat that is able to travel underwater. Change 1.
4 Shrub	A plant with woody stems that branch out close to the ground. Also called a bush. Add 2.
5 Rub	To use pressure on a surface with a back-and-forth motion. Take away 2.
6 Cub	A young bear. Change 1.
7 Cab	Another name for a taxi. Change 1.
8 Calm	Not moving, still. Replace last letter with 2.
9 Call	To say or shout in a loud voice. Change 1.
10 Fall	The season that comes after summer. Change 1.

Marjorie Maddox

Something about Marjorie Maddox

"Hiya!" That's how some folks say "Hello" in Pennsylvania, where I now live. In Ohio, where I grew up, people say, "Hey, there!" "What's up?" or "Hi, guys!" the latter for both girls and boys, kinda like "Y'all" in the South! How do you greet your friends?

When I was your age, I attended Evening Street Elementary School in Worthington, Ohio. Recently, my sister and I went back to visit. We're both curious like that. We just knocked on the principal's door and introduced ourselves. Boy, was she nice! She showed us all around and even gave us T-shirts left over from the school's recent fiftieth year celebration. And guess what we found in a dusty room marked ARCHIVES? My class photos from third, fourth, and fifth grades! No kidding! There I was with all my school friends. In one of the photos, I had a big bow in my hair. I remember that year well. It was fifth grade, and each afternoon our teacher, Mrs. Parks, read us a chapter from Madeleine L'Engle's *A Wrinkle in Time*. At the end of the year, she wrote a story where everyone in the class was a character, and we were "tessering" across space just like courageous Meg did in *A Wrinkle in Time*. It was great fun being a character in my teacher's story. It was even more fun making up stories and poems myself. As you've probably guessed, I still do it today!

Madeleine L'Engle's *A Wrinkle in Time* remains one of my favorite books. When I was older and at Wheaton College, I even got to take a class with the author. How cool is that? I studied writing and literature at Wheaton and earned a Master's and an MFA in Poetry Writing at the University of Louisville and Cornell University. Is that when I started writing, though? Nope! It was way before that, younger than you are now. I used to carry around a journal everywhere I went, writing stories and poems. I even published my first poem in *Campfire Girl Magazine* when I was eight. I was lucky; my parents thought writing was pretty awesome. My mom even typed up my stories and made them into a book.

If you, too, like to make up stories and poems, I'm right here cheering you on! If you haven't tried it yet, what are you waiting for? You can write about every and anything. I do! Baseball (my great granduncle was Branch Rickey, a friend to Jackie Robinson), animals, family, spelling (seriously, words are like magic tricks), what's inside of our bodies (also cool), what's outside in nature (Did you ever look closely at marching ants?), colors, art, music, and so much more.

Here's a more formal list of activities, the kind grown-ups like to have. It's still me, though, having fun with writing!

Bio: Professor of English and Creative Writing at Lock Haven University for over 30 years, Marjorie Maddox has published five children's and MG/YA books, including *A Crossing of Zebras: Animal Packs in Poetry*; *Rules of the Game: Baseball Poems*; the 2021 NCTE Notable Poetry Book *I'm Feeling Blue, Too!*; *Inside Out: Poems on Writing and Reading Poems with Insider Exercises* (Finalist International Book Award); and *How Can I Look It Up When I Don't Know How It's Spelled? Spelling Mnemonics and Grammar Tricks*. In addition, she has published over 15 collections of poetry for adults, a book of short stories, and the anthologies, with Jerry Wemple, *Common Wealth: Contemporary Poets on Pennsylvania* and *Keystone: Contemporary Poets on Pennsylvania* (PSU Press). The Assistant Editor of the literary journal *Presence* and the 2023–2024 radio host of WPSU's "Poetry Moment," she gives school visits, readings, and workshops around the world. Find out more at www.marjoriemaddox.com.

A Poem by Marjorie Maddox

How many of you LOVE animals? How many of you LOVE words? Your love of words + your love (or dislike) of anything else can = a poem. Here's what I mean. I love the idea of collective nouns, words that describe a group of animals, objects, or things. You've probably heard the phrase *a school of fish*. Did you know that a group of rattlesnakes is called a *rumba*, a type of dance? Snakes dancing?! Whether you like or dislike snakes, try picturing that! Now go a step further and act out the below poem. Be loud! I want to hear you clear over here in Pennsylvania!

A RUMBA OF RATTLESNAKES

A rumba of rattlesnakes knows how to shake
their long, slinky bodies and twist till daybreak.
They wobble their heads, give their hips a quick quake.
They jitterbug tails till their skeletons ache.

They rattle maracas and *rat-tat* on drums,
blow on tin trumpets, uncurl their tongues
to hiss a sweet song that invites you to come
a little bit closer. But you know to run
way over here and avoid the mistake
of dancing the rumba with ten rattlesnakes.

> This poem first appeared in *A Crossing of Zebras: Animal Packs in Poetry*, published by Wordsong/Boyds Mills Press in 2008. It was later republished by Wipf and Stock in 2019.

Feel like reading more don't-sit-still poems? You might enjoy my *I'm Feeling Blue, Too!* (Wipf and Stock, 2020) where a boy and his dog Blue turn the "can't-do-nothin' blues" into an exciting exploration of color. Or, if you like to watch or play sports, check out my book *Rules of the Game: Baseball Poems* (Reprinted by Wipf and Stock, 2019).

A Word Ladder by Timothy Rasinski

In a word ladder game, lead students from one word to the next by adding, subtracting, or changing one or a few letters from the previous word. Start at the top and work toward the bottom.

1 Snakes	Long narrow reptiles that have scales but no legs.
2 Shake	To move back and forth or up and down with quick motions. Change 1 and take away 1.
3 Shade	An area in which the sun's rays are blocked. Change 1.
4 Had	Past tense of "Have." Take away 2.
5 Mad	Another word for "angry." Change 1.
6 Mat	A piece of material that is used as a covering to protect a floor. Change 1.
7 Cat	A feline animal that is often a pet. Change 1.
8 Cattle	Large mammals raised on farms or ranches for their milk or meat. Add 3.
9 Battle	A fight between two armed forces in a war. Change 1.
10 Rattle	Combined with the first word to make a dangerous creature. Change 1.

Mary Lee Hahn

Something about Mary Lee Hahn

I did not become a poet because of a childhood filled with poetry books. I was not surrounded by adults who wrote and recited poems. I don't remember ever studying poetry in school.

I started becoming a poet at the same time I was learning to be a better teacher. In a Poetry for Children class taught by Dr. Charlotte Huck at The Ohio State University, we read piles and piles of poetry books and we were encouraged to write poetry ourselves. I used Gerard Manley Hopkins' *Pied Beauty* as a mentor text to write my own version, and climbing into his language, rhyme scheme, and meter taught me more about writing poetry than anything up to that point.

After receiving my Master's degree in Children's Literature at The Ohio State University, I taught fourth and fifth graders for 35 years and I read and wrote poetry alongside my students that whole time.

In 2006, when Franki Sibberson and I started our blog, A Year of Reading, my poetry writing moved to the next level. The blog gave me both a wider audience and, because Poetry Friday and the Kidlitosphere were also born in 2006, the blog gave me a community of writers. For the past 18 years, encouraged by that community, I have shared an original poem most weeks for Poetry Friday. For ten of those years, I've written and published a poem a day in April across a wide range of National Poetry Month projects.

Another boost to my poetry came with Janet Wong and Sylvia Vardell's Pomelo Books. I have poems published in four of their early Poetry Friday Anthologies, and in one of their more recent "Things We…" books. Those publications opened the door for my poems to be published in more than a dozen other anthologies.

Most recently, I joined two very different poetry critique groups. Learning to give and take constructive criticism and closely studying the poetry of my peers has helped me be a better poet.

Writing isn't my only creative outlet. I am also a fiber artist. I make art with embroidery, quilting, and block printing. I love baking cakes and bread And I'm a gardener, with a garden I've filled with plants that provide food for monarchs and black swallowtails, who I hand raise indoors and release when they emerge from their cocoons and are ready to fly.

Mary Lee Hahn is a poet, fiber artist, baker, and gardener. Her poems are in more than a dozen anthologies. Two she would highly recommend are National Geographic's *The Poetry of US* (edited by J. Patrick Lewis; National Geographic, 2018), and *Imperfect: Poems About Mistakes* (edited by Tabatha Yeatts; History House Publishers, 2018).

A Poem by Mary Lee Hahn

PERSEVERE IS A WORD

Persevere is a challenging word
containing none of the letters that spell luck.

The p throws down an anchor
and right from the beginning you're stuck.

Even though you might hesitate
with "er…"

"severe" comes along
tapping palm with ruler

goading you with a no-nonsense
frown-creased brow: *don't you dare quit,*

keep at it, try again,
summon up all your grit.

Just when you're about to throw in the towel,
"sever" chops the anchor rope

and sets you free. You did it! Your hard work paid off
and at least for now, it's a downhill slope.

A Word Ladder by Timothy Rasinski

In a word ladder game, lead students from one word to the next by adding, subtracting, or changing one or a few letters from the previous word. Start at the top and work toward the bottom.

1 Summon	A call to appear for a particular purpose.
2 Sum	The total of two or more numbers added together. Take away 3 letters.
3 Sun	The celestial object that produces heat and light. Change 1.
4 Sin	A religious term for a bad deed. Change 1
5 Sing	What you do with a song. Add 1
6 Ring	A piece of jewelry worn on the finger. Change 1.
7 Rind	The thick, firm outer layer or covering or oranges, lemons, and melons. Change 1.
8 Grind	To crush or make by crushing into very small pieces or a powder. Add 1.
9 Grin	Another name for a smile. Take away 1.
10 Grit	What the poet wants you to summon in the poem. Change 1

Maryfrances Wagner

Something about Maryfrances Wagner

Hi, All,

Many years ago, when I was a young girl, my mother used to write little poems and put them in my brother's, my father's, and my lunch boxes. She put them in with my father's camping gear when he went hunting and she put them in my brother's suitcase when he went to college. Sometimes little poems showed up on our pillows. We never knew when we were going to get one, so they were always a nice surprise.

My father sometimes wrote little poems for my mother and put them in her birthday and Valentine's Day cards, and when we were in the car going for ice cream or going to visit a relative, he'd recite poems he had memorized when he was in school, so I was surrounded by poetry early in life.

When I was in eighth grade, my teacher assigned us to write on country living even though we lived in the suburbs of Kansas City. My parents suggested I write a poem instead of an essay, so together we brainstormed ideas, and I went to my room and wrote a poem. My teacher liked it so much she had me read it out loud and put it in the school magazine. My journey writing poems had begun. While in high school, I started memorizing poems I loved – poems by Edgar Alan Poe, Robert Frost, and others.

I finally decided I needed to learn something about writing if I were going to take it seriously, so I went to college and took creative writing courses. I took many other classes as well including fencing, and I won first place in a regional fencing competition against eight colleges. I was so happy with my medal that I went dancing to celebrate. My Bachelor of Arts degree was in English, and my Master's degree focused on creative writing, and I kept on taking more courses in creative writing after that. Since then, I've published ten books of poetry, written many essays and reviews, and given many workshops and readings.

I taught creative writing and composition in high school and college, and I have taught and still teach creative writing workshops. I am the president of The Writers Place and an editor for a magazine called *I-70 Review*.

I've published poems in many magazines, was the Missouri State Finalist for Teacher of the Year, received the Thorpe Menn Book Award for my book *Red Silk*, was Missouri Individual Artist of the Year in 2020, and was Missouri Poet Laureate from 2021–2023, so my journey in writing poetry has been long and fulfilling.

I also love to grow flowers and vegetables, feed and watch birds, and walk along a path near the Little Blue River. I have two rescued dogs named Annie Sexton and Lucille Clifton. We always name our dogs after poets. They go with my husband Greg and me every day on our walks.

A Poem by Maryfrances Wagner

MORNING WALK

Small as a dime,
a frog springs
across my path,
settles in understory.

A garden snake
slides into sedge
when warm gravel
shifts and scatters.

A box turtle,
except for a nub
of nail, shuts
his doors.

I am the cause
of sudden
silence.

If you haven't already read them, I'd recommend you read *Frog and Toad Are Friends* (HarperCollins, 2003) and all the Frog and Toad books by Arnold Lobel. They teach the value of friendship. Staying on the subject of frogs, I also recommend the *Frog, Where Are You?* series by Mercer Mayer (Dial Books; Illustrated edition, 2003). Mayer shows he can tell a story without words at all.

A Word Ladder by Timothy Rasinski

In a word ladder game, lead students from one word to the next by adding, subtracting, or changing one or a few letters from the previous word. Start at the top and work toward the bottom.

1 Silence	Quiet – absence of noise.
2 Since	Another word for "because." Take away 2.
3 Wince	To draw suddenly back or away from something painful or frightening. Change 1.
4 Win	Opposite of lose. Take away 2.
5 Wink	To open and close one eye quickly. Add 1.
6 Pink	The color that comes from mixing red and white. Change 1.
7 Pin	Something that fastens to clothing by using a pointed piece of wire. Take away 1.
8 Pen	An instrument for writing or drawing with ink. Change 1.
9 Den	A comfortable, cozy room used for reading, watching TV, and other enjoyable activities. Change 1.
10 Sudden	Immediately, right now. Add 3.

Matt Forrest Esenwine

Something about Matt Forrest Esenwine

Believe it or not, I was once an elementary school student just like you! Well, maybe not "just" like you – I was autistic (still am, ha!) and I loved reading poetry, hanging out in the woods near our house, taking care of our horses, playing basketball and soccer, and reading lots and LOTS of comic books. Hmmm, perhaps we WERE alike, after all? My favorite superheroes were Spiderman and Ghost Rider but my favorite poets were Dorothy Aldis and Robert Frost – so I guess I had a love of beautiful language and powerful characters!

Speaking of favorites, here are a few of mine:

Meal: Pizza
Snack: Nachos
Dessert: Chocolate chip cookies
Ice cream: Phantomberry (black raspberry ice cream with fudge brownie pieces and a chocolate cookie crunch!)
Movie: Jurassic World or Spiderman 2 (the one with Doc Oc!)
Color: Dark green
Season: Summertime, baby!!

One of the things I love about poetry is that it's short and compact – you can say a lot in a little space. You can describe a scene, a feeling, or a pet in just a few short lines and then move on to something else! And for someone with a short attention span like me, that's perfect. I've been writing poems since I was about ten years old. I once wrote a five-page book of poems about trees for my mom, and I still have it!

So what have I written that you might have read? Well, quite a few things, actually! My debut picture book, *Flashlight Night* (Astra Young Readers, 2017), received lots of positive reviews including something super-special called a "Kirkus star," and it was even selected as one of New York Public Library's Best Books for Kids 2017. It also showed up on Encyclopedia Britannica's list of "11 Children's Books That Inspire Imagination," which I have to admit was pretty cool.

I now have nearly a dozen books to my credit including *I Am Today* (POW! Kids Books, 2022), which received the 2023 New Hampshire State Literary Award for Outstanding Children's Literature, and *Once Upon Another Time* (Beaming Books, 2021), a book I co-wrote with my friend Charles ("Father Goose®") Ghigna, which the American Library Association called "a necessary addition to picture book collections." Wow, what an honor, huh?

Meanwhile, my children's poetry can be found in poetry collections known as "anthologies" like *The National Geographic Book of Nature Poetry* (National Geographic Children's Books, 2015) and *Construction People* (Wordsong, 2020). I live in New Hampshire with my wife, kids, and more pets than I have fingers! Last time I counted, we had seven dogs, four cats, and a dozen chickens – but I should probably go double-check because that number could have changed in the past hour.

A Poem by Matt Forrest Esenwine

PEAS

I don't like peas. I really don't.
Yes, I should eat them – but I won't.
They're very tasty, so I'm told,
but I would rather eat green mold
on slimy yogurt six months old
while standing naked in the cold
than even *think* of eating peas,
so please don't ask me, please, oh please.
I'd rather chew a garden hose
or dine on tiny termite toes –
or even what's inside their nose –
than have this meal which you propose.
I've been quite clear just where I stand;
I hate them frozen, fresh, or canned.
I'll eat the gum stuck on your shoe,
an orange that is turning blue,
some homemade caterpillar stew
with rancid tripe and haggis, too;
I might chow down on all of these,
but I really…
 …really…
  …don't like peas.

This is the first time this poem has ever been published in a book – which means YOU are one of the very first people to have ever read it! I hope you liked it and maybe even chuckled a little bit.

Two other books I've written that you might enjoy (in addition to the three I mentioned earlier) are *Don't Ask a Dinosaur* (POW! Kids Books, 2018), about 14 dinosaurs trying to put on a birthday party and failing miserably, and *The Thing to Remember about Stargazing* (Tilbury House, 2023), a book that celebrates the joy of spending quiet time with yourself and the stars at night. At the end of this book, you'll find a long list of titles by the poets in *40 Poems for 40 Weeks* plus many others.

A Word Ladder by Timothy Rasinski

In a word ladder game, lead students from one word to the next by adding, subtracting, or changing one or a few letters from the previous word. Start at the top and work toward the bottom.

1 Green	A color.
2 Grin	To smile. Replace 2 vowels with 1.
3 Grind	To crush into very small pieces or a powder. Add 1.
4 Rind	The outer layer or covering of oranges and lemons. Take away 1.
5 Bind	To tie together with rope or cord. Change 1.
6 Mind	The part of a person that thinks. Change 1.
7 Mine	Something that belongs to you is _____. Change 1.
8 Mile	A distance of 5,280 feet. Change 1.
9 Mild	Gentle or calm. Change 1.
10 Mold	Combine with first word to make what the poet would rather eat besides peas. Change 1.

Michael Salinger

Something about Michael Salinger

Hiya Writers and Readers,

I've always loved to read and write myself from as long as I can remember – which is a very long time. I've actually been a published poet for over 50 years.

When I was in fourth grade my teacher sent a poem I wrote about monsters going to a birthday party to *Scholastic Magazine*. They used to take student submissions back then. Well, they published my poem in the student section, and I was a published poet! I didn't get my second poem published in a national magazine until I was around 23 years old – I had a little lag in my publishing career.

As I continued in school after fourth grade, I found a few series books that really captured my imagination. First early on, *Encyclopedia Brown*, then when I was in middle school, I started reading a fantasy series *Conan the Barbarian*. Once I got a bit older, I started looking for the same author on a book after I had read one by them that I liked. So instead of series I started following authors.

I went to a state university and once I left there I worked as an engineer for 23 years. But while I was working as an engineer I continued to read and write. A big part of my job as an engineer was writing. It was technical writing, like instructions on how to do different jobs. The cool thing though is I continued writing poetry on the side as a hobby. Here's something interesting, as my poetry got better so did my work writing. All the tricks I was learning and using to write and recite poetry made me a better overall communicator!

Then, finally I was able to make poetry my full-time job by teaching others how to write and speak better. Nowadays I travel all over the world – over 62 countries last count! – talking with teachers and students about strategies to improve their writing and speaking and it is the best job ever.

A Poem by Michael Salinger

MONKEYSHINES

Do not feed the monkey!
Don't look him in the eye.
Don't smile,
even if you're happy.
Let me tell you why.
Monkeys are greedy
and bad company.
One treat won't satisfy.
If you feed the monkey,
monkeys are not shy.
They reach into your pockets,
pry your glasses
from your eyes.
They've got sticky little fingers.
You can kiss your bananas goodbye.
Do not feed the monkey.
Don't look him in the eye.

A Word Ladder by Timothy Rasinski

In a word ladder game, lead students from one word to the next by adding, subtracting, or changing one or a few letters from the previous word. Start at the top and work toward the bottom.

1 Reach	To grab for something.
2 Peach	A fruit. Change 1.
3 Peace	Opposite of war. Change 1.
4 Pea	A green vegetable. Take away 2.
5 Peak	The top part of a mountain. Add 1.
6 Peek	To look quickly or secretly. Change 1.
7 Seek	To look for something. Change 1.
8 Sock	A cloth covering for the foot. Change the middle 2 letters.
9 Socket	An opening into which something fits or is put. Add 2.
10 Pockets	What the poet says monkeys will reach into. Change first letter and add 1.

Nancy Bo Flood

Something about Nancy Bo Flood

I love stories. Reading and writing them. Stories help open our hearts, heal our hearts, and give us new eyes to see the world.

In college I wanted to learn about the brain. How do we remember; why do we forget; how does our brain work – or not work? So I became a "fish-brain surgeon," a research neuropsychologist, and studied the brains of fish. Why fish? Because their brains are simple but their ability to learn and remember is complex. Brain research might seem like a long way from writing books for kids, but it is not.

I write to share experiences and information that is exciting… or sometimes sad. I love rodeo and learned that on the Navajo Nation, rodeo is not just riding a bucking bronco to win a medal. Rodeo is about working together, learning practical ranching skills, understanding and taking care of animals. So I wrote *Cowboy Up: Ride the Navajo Rodeo.* Poetry about rodeo was fun to write and is full of excitement!

Dance is also important to me. Dance is one way of expressing thoughts and feelings, or telling a story. Everyone should be able to dance, even if you can't move your legs. So I wrote *I Will Dance,* a true story about a girl who could only move her head and hands but her one wish was to dance. And she did.

Stories – however they are written – allow us to feel what it is like to be someone else, to understand kids living in different situations. Story has the power to help us imagine, to dream, to wonder. And even laugh out loud.

My "bottom line" message: Read anything and everything. You learn interesting stuff, meet interesting people, and go places you have never been. Read every day! As a kid, I kept a stack of comic books under my bed. And a flashlight! Now I keep a stack of books next to my bed. You never know when you need a good book.

My books have received a variety of awards, national and international. To learn more about my work, please browse through my website www.nancyboflood.com.

A Poem by Nancy Bo Flood

DOUBLE BUBBLE GUM TROUBLE

I chewed
And chewed
Then
Blew and blew.
My bubble grew…
And Grew … and … GREW

Until

POP!

Oh, No.
It's on my nose
It's in my hair
Double Bubble *everywhere.*

Piece by piece
I peel off pink.

Ooops

DROPPED
    D
      D it.

All gone?

Wrong.

Ugh.

Now
My shoe,

Stuck!

Yuck.

A Word Ladder by Timothy Rasinski

In a word ladder game, lead students from one word to the next by adding, subtracting, or changing one or a few letters from the previous word. Start at the top and work toward the bottom.

1 Every	Each and all parts of a group of people or things.
2 Very	A word used to make an adjective stronger. Take away 1.
3 Verb	A word that expresses action. Change 1.
4 Herb	A plant that adds flavor to food. Change 1.
5 He	A male pronoun. Take away 2.
6 Hi	An informal way of saying hello. Change 1.
7 Hive	A structure in which bees live. Add 2.
8 Hire	To take on someone as a worker for pay. Change 1.
9 Here	The opposite of elsewhere. "Not there, but _____." Change 1.
10 Where	Referring to a particular location. Combine with first word to make a word that means in all places. Add 1.

Nikki Grimes

Something about Nikki Grimes

I've been writing since I was six years old. I've always loved that one word can mean many different things, and that words are so powerful, you can write something funny, and a person a thousand miles away can read it and laugh!

I was born in Harlem, New York, but my poems have taken me across the country, and around the world. I've been to the Library of Congress, the White House, and to schools from coast to coast. I've shared my poetry and stories with audiences in China, Tanzania, Sweden, Ireland, and, most recently, in Singapore, where I got to meet students just like you.

Many of my books are written in poems, including my novels *Words with Wings* and *Garvey's Choice*. Even my books of nonfiction, like *Talkin' About Bessie,* and *Kamala Harris: Rooted in Justice*, are written in lyrical verse. Poetry is simply my favorite thing! I hope someday it will be yours, too.

A Poem by Nikki Grimes

JAZZY LEGS

The stars on my stockings
should give you a hint.
Some day, I'll be famous.
I'll be worth a mint.

I'll outshine each actress
Who's ever been seen.
I'll master the great stage,
and light the big screen.

Don't worry. I'll leave room
for you at the top.
But once you start climbing,
make sure you don't stop.

Meanwhile, find some stockings
that tell who you are.
The world looks at me and
they *know* I'm a star.

A Word Ladder by Timothy Rasinski

In a word ladder game, lead students from one word to the next by adding, subtracting, or changing one or a few letters from the previous word. Start at the top and work toward the bottom.

1 Famous	A person recognized or liked by the public.
2 Mouse	A small rodent. Delete first 2 letters and add 1.
3 House	A building in which families live. Change 1.
4 Hose	A flexible tube of rubber or plastic that carries water or liquid from one place to another. Take away 1.
5 Shoe	A protective covering for a human foot. Rearrange the letters
6 Shove	To push. Add 1.
7 Stove	A device that uses electricity or burns fuel to provide heat for cooking or warmth. Change 1.
8 Store	A place where things are sold. Also, a supply of something for future use. Change 1.
9 Stare	To look intently at something or someone. Change 1
10 Star	What the poet says she is. Take away 1

Nile Stanley

Something about Nile Stanley

Teachers call me Dr. Nile Stanley, but kids everywhere know me as "Nile Crocodile, the reading reptile." I am a poet and professor who ignites a passion for reading. I love to visit schools and get the "word" to the herd!

Poetry helps kids learn to read. Poetry is a treasure, rarer than gold. It's precious feelings you can hold. Acting out poetry, raps, stories, songs, and dances (cha-cha-cha) make learning fun. Poetry travels well and helps me make new friends. I've performed poetry in every land: Canada, England, Germany, Alaska to Nebraska, Vietnam, and even Wuhan, China. So do your school a favor and share a poem with your neighbor.

Nile Stanley Biography for Adults

Nile Stanley, Ph.D. is an Associate Professor of Literacy and Arts Education at the University of North Florida, Jacksonville. He is a founding board member of Hope at Hand, Inc., a non-profit organization that provides poetry and arts interventions for underserved youth.

He is a member of the editorial board for the *Journal of Poetry Therapy*. He chaired the International Literacy Association's (ILA) annual poetry olio gathering for 20 years. He is an artist-in-residence for schools, funded by gifts from the Cummer Family Foundation. Dr. Stanley's numerous books and articles have focused on using poetry and storytelling for literacy instruction and building resilience. Nile has been a visiting scholar to Alaska, China, Germany, Trinidad, and Vietnam.

Recommended books:

Creating Readers with Poetry by Nile Stanley (Maupin House, 2004).

Performance Literacy Through Storytelling by Nile Stanley and Brett Dillingham (Maupin House, 2009).

A Poem by Nile Stanley

WORDS

I like to say them
like *jitterbug,*
fudge,
and *tangerine.*

Words

I like to play with them
like hacky sacks,
catching and bouncing them
off my tongue.

Words

I like to
weigh them
like
bittersweet. and *jumbo shrimp.*

Words

Most of all
I like to devour them slowly,
savoring each sound.

Words

Yum! Words give me power; words give me knowledge.
Knowing lots of words prepared me for college.

Words

The more I know, the more I learn.
This has an effect on what I earn!

A Word Ladder by Timothy Rasinski

In a word ladder game, lead students from one word to the next by adding, subtracting, or changing one or a few letters from the previous word. Start at the top and work toward the bottom.

1 Knowledge	Understanding of one or more topics.
2 Ledge	A shelf of rock coming out from a wall or cliff. Take away 4.
3 Hedge	A solid row of bushes used as a fence. Change 1.
4 Edge	The border or outside line of something. Take away 1.
5 Egg	A food produced by chicken. Take away 2 and add 1.
6 Peg	A small piece of wood or other material used to hold things together. Take away 1 letter and add 1.
7 Pew	A bench or type of seating found in churches and places of worship. Change 1.
8 Pow	A loud sound or explosion. Change 1.
9 Powder	Fine, loose grains that are made when a solid material has been ground or crushed. Add 3.
10 Power	Besides knowledge, what words give you. Take away 1 letter.

Rebecca Dotlich

Something about Rebecca Dotlich

If you have a minute, I'd like to tell you that my name is Rebecca (I wonder what yours is!) and I'm a word collector. I'm also a scribbler, a journal and notebook keeper, and a poet and picture book author. I grew up in Indiana, and spent my days ice skating on ponds, building snow forts, riding my bike on trails by the creek, and reading comic books & mysteries.

I had an older brother who loved to read books like *Treasure Island* and any books about dinosaurs and faraway countries and shipwrecks. I had a younger sister who was born when I was five and was in the hospital for almost a year before she could come home. When she did, you can believe we all hovered over her, and I was often in charge of looking out for her.

My favorite food when I was young was warm pot pies my mom would buy frozen and put in the oven for us. And spaghetti. And hot cocoa with marshmallows. And she'd bake the best cherry pies and applesauce spice cakes. I remember piling in the back of our station wagon and going to the movies outside, called drive-ins with big outdoor screens. We put on plays in our backyard and jumped rope and played kickball until the streetlights came on. I sure miss those days.

After high school I went to college at Indiana University in Bloomington, Indiana, where I studied creative writing, anthropology, and art history. I took a lot of songwriting and poetry classes, too. The only thing I ever really wanted to be was a writer. I have now published many children's poetry and picture books, maybe about 30 or more. I've had poems featured on *Reading Rainbow* and you might see my name sometime in magazines you'll see in school, like *Storyworks* or *Scope*, and in textbooks and anthologies. My books have been awarded a Boston Globe Horn Book Honor, a Golden Kite picture book Honor, a Bank Street Best Book of the Year, 10 Best Books for Babies, Indiana Best Read Aloud, a Gold Oppenheim Toy Portfolio Award, and a Subaru SB&F Prize finalist. *The Knowing Book* has been compared to the famous graduation gift book *Oh, The Places You'll Go* by independent bookstore owners.

I have visited hundreds of classrooms across the country, and I love to teach poetry workshops to writers, teachers, and students. I have been a contributing columnist and poetry advisor to *Creative Classroom* magazine and *Teaching K-8* and have served twice on the NCTE Award for Excellence in Poetry Committee, the Lee Bennett Hopkins Poetry Award through Penn State, and The International Reading Association's Committee on Poetry & Prose Awards.

I still live in Indiana, I still love warm pot pies and spaghetti, and I am pretty good at baking and icing cookies in the shapes of bells and stars at Christmastime. But what I love most is writing. I spend most of my time in my writing room filled with vintage typewriters and small toys like miniature cars and trolls, marbles, coins, keys, and jacks in all colors. I can't have enough school supplies: colorful notecards, notepads, and folders. And books! Piles of books! If you'd like to know more about me, you can take a look at my website, even though it needs updating – something writers don't always take the time to do. www.rebeccakaidotlich.com

A Poem by Rebecca Dotlich

ROOM OF MYSTERY

What was it like
that final day
when all you knew
fell away,

and dinosaur roars,
one by one
went silent, and
then did the sun
explode upon the Earth
that day, a searing sort
of cinder-spray;
and did the world
turn ember blue
as flakes of ash
blew down on you
as meteors
from outer space
sprayed hot pebbles
in your face
and cauterized your tails gray;
what was it *like*
that final day?

This poem is from *Welcome to the Wonder House,* a Wordsong book published by Astra Books for Young Readers (2023).

A few other books of mine that you might like: *One Day, The End* (Astra Young Readers, 2021), *When Riddles Come Rumbling* (Wordsong; Illustrated edition, 2013), and *Lemonade Sun* (Wordsong, 1998).

A Word Ladder by Timothy Rasinski

In a word ladder game, lead students from one word to the next by adding, subtracting, or changing one or a few letters from the previous word. Start at the top and work toward the bottom.

1 Space	Area that contains the entire universe beyond the Earth.
2 Spare	An item that is put aside for future use. Change 1
3 Spire	A tall, narrow, upward structure shaped like a cone on the outside of a building; steeple. Change 1.
4 Spirit	The way a person feels or thinks, as marked by qualities such as courage or energy. Replace last letter with 2.
5 Sport	Athletic event or game played according to rules. Replace two letters with 1.
6 Spot	A mark, such as a stain, different in color from the area around it. Take away 1.
7 Pot	A kitchen utensil used for boiling water. Take away 1.
8 Pout	To show unhappy feelings with an expression of the face. Add 1.
9 Pouter	One who pouts. Add 2.
10 Outer	Combine with first word to describe where the meteors came from. Take away 1.

Renée LaTulippe

Something about Renée LaTulippe

Hello, readers! I'm Renée and I grew up in upstate New York in a small town with a people population of 2,000 and a cow population of 10,000, give or take a moo or two. I have lots of great memories of growing up in the country: hiking up the hill to our tree fort, ice skating on the flooded and frozen cornfield across the street, jumping into the river from the old covered bridge, and lots of long summer bike rides on long winding paths.

It turns out I really liked winding paths, and I traveled a lot of them over the years. One path led me to poetry. Yup, I became a poet at the ripe old age of seven with my first poem called "Whale in the Sea." Do you think it's weird that I was surrounded by cows and pastures but my first poems were all about whales and jellyfish? No matter – I just kept writing and writing and writing all through elementary school and middle school and high school and college and … well, you get the picture.

Another path led me to the theater, which led to an even longer path that took me right out of the country and into New York City to study acting and directing. I stayed there a good long time, too. You might be wondering if I missed the cows. I did, because cows are adorable. But being on stage was a thrill, and I knew the cows would understand.

But those paths were always calling my name, so I took another one and became a teacher of English and theater … until yet *another* path beckoned me to move to Italy and be a writer (and that was a REALLY wet path, let me tell you). And here I am now, a writer living by the Mediterranean Sea, where it finally makes sense to write poems about whales and jellyfish!

I'm so glad to have met you along my path!

Now here's an "official" list of some of the writerly things I do:

Renée M. LaTulippe is the author of the poem picture book *The Crab Ballet* and the forthcoming poetry collection *Limelight: Theater Poems to Perform*. She also has poems published in many anthologies including *No World Too Big, Night Wishes, School

People, National Geographic's *The Poetry of US* and *Book of Nature Poetry, One Minute Till Bedtime, ThankU: Poems of Gratitude*, and others. In the educational market, Renée has co-authored nine award-winning decodable readers and a collection of poetry. Renée developed and teaches the online course The Lyrical Language Lab and provides free writing lessons for children's writers on her YouTube channel. She earned her BFA in acting/directing from Marymount Manhattan College and her MA in English Education from New York University.

A Poem by Renée LaTulippe

I love learning how people lived and worked in the past. The 1930s was a difficult time for many families in America, especially farmers who endured the hardships of the Great Depression and the Dust Bowl. This poem is inspired by those families.

CHILD'S CHANT

Oklahoma Dust Bowl, 1935

Dust blows in, dust blows out.
Drought brings dust, dust brings drought.
    Right hand in, swirl about—
    dust blows in, dust blows out.

Bury scarecrow, bury cow,
bury chickens, bury plow.
    Dust blows in, dust blows out—
    left hand in, swirl about.

Papa fiddles, baby cries,
Mama stares at empty skies.
    Right foot in, swirl about—
    dust blows in, dust blows out.

Dust for breakfast, dust for dinner.
Crops stop growing, hope grows thinner.
    Dust blows in, dust blows out—
    left foot in, swirl about.

Packed jalopy, laden mule.
Goodbye friends, goodbye school.
    Whole self in, swirl about—
    dust blows in; we blow out.

A Word Ladder by Timothy Rasinski

In a word ladder game, lead students from one word to the next by adding, subtracting, or changing one or a few letters from the previous word. Start at the top and work toward the bottom.

1 Dust	Dry tiny pieces of soil or dirt.
2 Rust	An orange or reddish-brown coating that forms on metal that has been exposed to air and water. Change 1.
3 Crust	The slightly hard, baked dough on the outside of bread or pies. Add 1.
4 Crow	A shiny black bird known for its shrill, harsh cry. Also, to brag. Replace last 3 letters with 2.
5 Row	A method for moving or propelling a boat. Take away 1.
6 Grow	To become larger by natural development. Add 1
7 Flow	To move in a smooth, steady stream. Change first 2.
8 Follow	To go behind someone when moving. Add 2.
9 Low	Opposite of high. Take away 3.
10 Blows	What the poet says that the wind does. Add 1 letter to the beginning and 1 to the end.

Sandy Asher

Something about Sandy Asher

I can remember writing as far back as second grade. I may have been writing before then. I know I was making up poems, stories, and plays long before I knew how to write them down. I loved to read and to be read to by family members and teachers. I imagined it would be the most wonderful thing in the world to create poems, stories, and plays that someone would love as much as I loved those I read and heard.

Back there in second grade, I made up short plays and acted them out with my friends. Our teacher invited us to perform for the class, and even sent us on tour around the school to perform for other classes. All through my school years, teachers encouraged me to keep on writing and to share what I'd written. I've always been grateful for their belief in my ability.

I didn't know you could get paid for writing until I read Louisa May Alcott's book, *Little Women*. That was around fifth grade or so. Until then, arranging words in interesting ways was kind of a game I enjoyed playing. But Alcott's main character, Jo March, who grew up writing, just as I did, was determined to publish her stories and get paid for them. That inspired me to do the same.

The very first poem I published was one that I wrote for an assignment in a college class and bravely mailed out to a literary journal. Just before winter break of my senior year, I received a postcard telling me the poem would appear in a future issue. I was thrilled!

That was the beginning. Since then, I've published dozens of poems, along with short stories, articles, and plays, in many literary journals, magazines, and anthologies. I've also published more than two dozen books for young readers, including *Too Many Frogs!*, *Chicken Story Time*, and *Sophie's Monster Goes to Shul*. I've edited collections of work by other writers, too, such as *Writing It Right: How Successful Children's Authors Revise and Sell Their Stories* and *With All My Heart, With All My Mind: 13 Stories about Growing Up Jewish*, winner of the National Jewish Book Award in children's literature.

As "Sandra Fenichel Asher," I've written more than three dozen plays for young and adult audiences. They've been produced nationwide and abroad, including Canada, England, Ireland, Scotland, Pakistan, South Korea, the Czech Republic, Australia, and New Zealand.

It's been a great joy to create and lead writing workshops for young people and adults all across the country. It was a special honor to serve as the first Lancaster Children's Laureate appointed by the Lancaster Literary Guild.

I live in Lancaster, PA, with my husband, Harvey; our dog, Gracie; and our cat, Friday. I hope you'll visit me at http://sandyasher.com.

A Poem by Sandy Asher

HOW DID SHE KNOW?

"Here, try this book," the librarian said.
"I think it's one you'll like."
Didn't want to hurt her feelings
so I pedaled it home on my bike.
Cover was ugly.
Print was small.
Too many pages.
No pictures at all
The story happened
a long time ago
in a place I've never heard of
to people I don't know.
No sports.
No dogs
No ghosts.
No jokes.
Sure to be a bore.
It wasn't like a single book
I'd ever read before.
What made her think I'd like it,
Out of all the kids in town?
And how come, once I started,
I couldn't put it down?

A Word Ladder by Timothy Rasinski

In a word ladder game, lead students from one word to the next by adding, subtracting, or changing one or a few letters from the previous word. Start at the top and work toward the bottom.

1 Put	To move something to a particular place.
2 Pit	A hole in the ground. Change 1.
3 It	A pronoun that refers to a thing, animal, person, or object that has been mentioned. Take away 1.
4 Hit	To strike. Add 1.
5 Hot	Very warm. Change 1.
6 How	When meeting someone new you might say "_____ do you do." Change 1.
7 Chow	Food for eating. Add 1.
8 Crow	Shiny black bird known for its shrill, harsh cry. Change 1.
9 Crown	A headpiece worn by a king or queen. Add 1.
10 Down	Combine with #1 and #3 to describe what the author could not do with the book. Replace first 2 letters with 1.

Sara Holbrook

Something about Sara Holbrook

I guess you could say, I'm a little bit ornery. In fact, a lot of my poems have been written when I should be doing something else. I used to work in corporate communications, a job I quit to become a poet. Truth was, I'd been secretly writing poems at my desk instead of writing press releases for years.

Still, when I changed professions, it scared a lot of my friends and even my daughters. But one thing I knew is that poetry is powerful language, and writing all those poems when I was supposed to be doing something else had actually helped all my writing, including the speeches, articles, and brochures.

Since embarking on my career as a poet, I have carried the message about the power of poetry to (by last count) 62 different countries around the globe and 48 States. I am the author of poetry books for kids, teens, and adults, and believe that poetry is best when it is shared aloud. I have also written five books for teachers and one novel, *The Enemy: Detroit 1954*, which won the Jane Addams Peace Prize. I feel I am living proof that poetry can take you places you can never say you've never been before again.

A Poem by Sara Holbrook

ONE OF A KIND

Unique is one of a kind,
no question.
It's not like anything else.
Whether quiet
or quirky,
sleepy
or perky,
Unique is something to see.
Equipped with exceptional talents,
I have to say,
"Unique is me."

A Word Ladder by Timothy Rasinski

In a word ladder game, lead students from one word to the next by adding, subtracting, or changing one or a few letters from the previous word. Start at the top and work toward the bottom.

1 Unique	One of a kind.
2 Unit	A single thing that is one of a group of similar things. Replace 3 letters with 1.
3 Unfit	Not suitable or appropriate for some purpose. Add 1.
4 Fit	To be in good health. Take away 2.
5 Fist	When fingers are balled up you make this. Add 1.
6 Fast	Opposite of slow. Change 1.
7 Last	Opposite of first. Change 1.
8 Lash	A whip or the striking part of a whip. Change 1.
9 Flash	A sudden, bright light that shines, then quickly disappears. Add 1.
10 Flesh	Another name for our skin. Change 1.
11 Mesh	A material or article made of fiber woven to form open spaces, as in a net. Replace first 2 letters with 1.
12 Me	A person who the author says is unique. Take away 2.

Ted Kooser

Something about Ted Kooser

I was in third grade so very many years ago that not only is my school gone, torn down and replaced by another, but every house I walked past between my house and the school has a different family living there, different dogs barking, different cats sitting inside the windows looking out at the birds. Change, as you'll learn as you grow older, is relentless, and never lets up. There isn't anything that isn't changing, sometimes quite quickly, at other times very slowly.

The tectonic plates that make up the great continents of the Earth are among the things that move very, very slowly. A tectonic plate moves at the same speed that our fingernails and toenails grow, no faster than that.

So I am a poet who writes about change, and about Time, and about something that has a good word for it, mutability. Mutability is about how everything is on its way into the past. Wherever you look you can see mutability. A flower you picked just yesterday has already begun to change. A pencil you put in your shirt pocket isn't, today, the same pencil it was yesterday. Something about it is different. It looks like the same pencil but everything all around it is in a slightly different place. Has the pencil changed or the place for the pencil?

As a poet I write about things like that, things that are changing, that are passing away, or that are becoming something that they'll be for a while. It's my job to try to keep things with us for a while longer. I have published lots of poems, and books of poems, and other books, too, five books for children, with illustrations, two books about being a writer, another book about where I live in Nebraska. All of those books are trying to preserve something, maybe just a story. I have been lucky to find people who like to read what I've written.

When I was a third grader I wasn't much good at sports, and I was one of the last kids to get chosen to be on a team. I wasn't good at music, either, though my parents paid for piano lessons for a while. But I could draw and I liked telling stories and writing poems. We all tend to stick with what we're good at, and

I've been writing and drawing for 80 years, and I never made a goal in soccer, or a touchdown in football, or won a foot race. But I kept writing and writing and writing, and eventually somebody noticed that I was pretty good at it. If you practice long enough at one activity, you can get really good at it. If I hadn't chosen writing, I might have chosen to be good with a bow and arrow. And if I had practiced long enough, today I could put a hundred arrows right into a bull's eye from 50 yards out.

So I encourage you to find what you like to do and to enjoy that, no matter what it is, and not to worry if you aren't doing what everyone else is doing. And to keep at it, day by day, knowing that eventually you'll get really good at it, and other people will notice and say, "That kid over there is really good at playing the harmonica."

A Poem by Ted Kooser

THE STORY OF AN APPLE TREE

An apple tree high on a hill and pithy with age
toppled over, and as it fell it flung out one
last apple, tough as a baseball, and it bounced
downhill and rolled and stopped against a rock

where over the winter it came apart at the seams
and spilled its seeds. And one of the seeds found
a damp spot under the side and sprouted there,
and soon, by the measurements of sky and clouds,

it became a tiny apple tree that was already
trying to elbow the rock aside. And there it grew,
wild in the wind down the hill, scattering petals,
white with pink centers, with pea-sized knobs

behind those blossoms that by summer would be
apples. And the tree grew and grew, and grew
even more, and thousands of honeybees came
and went, and in winter deer scuffed in the snow

for the apples it dropped, but the tree grew old
and weak, as had the first tree, and it fell,
and one of its leathery apples rolled downhill,
and lay patiently under the snow where the deer

couldn't find it, and in the spring it also sprouted
becoming a tree, just a small one, but with hope,
and it grew there, a hundred feet down the slope
from the original tree, which by then was no more

than a damp brown heap of bark and branches,
and this cycle continued, each apple sapling
lifting out of the skin of the last apple, and each
sprouting a few more yards downhill until

maybe a dozen generations later, an apple tree
came up at the foot of the hill where they'd all
been going, and it leaned against an old stone wall
at a meadow's edge, pushing against the wall

but not able to move it, and that tree too,
as it grew, dropped its fruit in the long grass
around it, the deer coming far down the hill
to find them there, and then finally, as a very,

very old tree soon to lie in the shade
it bent over its very last apple, dropped over
the wall, and what was the name of that tree?
It was called the Seek-No-Further, and a man

named Eric Sloane found one of the last ones,
though you might seek and find one, too, at the foot
of a wall, still young with maybe two leaves only,
open like hands, on the warm sunny side.

> Loosely based on a passage from Eric
> Sloane's book, *A Reverence for Wood*,
> Wilfred Funk, Inc., New York, 1965.

A Word Ladder by Timothy Rasinski

In a word ladder game, lead students from one word to the next by adding, subtracting, or changing one or a few letters from the previous word. Start at the top and work toward the bottom.

1 Apple	A fruit that is harvested in the autumn.
2 Grapple	To struggle to master a difficult object or problem. Add 2.
3 Grape	A small, juicy fruit, with a smooth skin that is either green, red, or purple. Take away 2.
4 Grace	A prayer that is said before meals. Change 1.
5 Grate	A frame of crossed or parallel metal bars used as a covering or guard over an opening. Change 1.
6 Late	Opposite of early. Replace first 2 letters with 1.
7 Flat	When tires lose air they are called _____. Add 1 letter to beginning and take away a letter from the end.
8 Flee	To run away. Change last 2.
9 Free	Not held back or confined. Change 1.
10 Tree	What apples grow on. Change 1

Wyatt Townley

Something about Wyatt Townley

I'm Wyatt, a girl who's tall for her age, especially when I climb trees (see photo). When I was little – okay, I was never *little*, but when I was young, much younger than you are – a bad thing happened to me. I wasn't able to talk to anyone about it until I grew up, but it got me writing early on, and I've written poetry ever since.

I was a lonely child, and sometimes it seemed like the page was the only friend I had. I would lie on my bed and scribble for hours. Those hours didn't go to waste, because they helped me discover my own way of looking at the world. That is called finding your voice, and it gets stronger with use, just like a muscle.

Alongside the writing, I became a dancer, because I like to do impossible things. My body was comical for dancing – pigeon-toed, flat-footed, taller than all the other kids in school. Once I advanced to toe shoes, dancing *en pointe* made me 7-feet tall!

Nevertheless, I persisted. I danced with the Missouri Dance Theatre, then moved to New York to study at a conservatory, where I graduated with a performing arts degree. I went on to dance professionally and direct my own dance company. Once I had the role of a lifetime: for the entire dance, my feet never touched down! As the soloist, I was passed and tossed from one partner to many partners – and at the climactic moment, they hurled my 6'2" body 15 feet into the air. In dress rehearsal before opening night, the group that was running to catch me ran a few inches too far. Upside down and headfirst, I hit the floor. I broke my neck. The doctors said I would never dance again. They were wrong!

After recovering, I returned to the stage even stronger. Meanwhile, I kept writing and publishing poems in magazines and journals. Eventually, enough poems were polished and published to make a book. I had found my path, and after writing more poems and more books, and doing many readings and tours, I was chosen to be the Poet Laureate of Kansas. They don't give you a crown or anything (I'm still waiting for the cape), but a title like that opens doors. I've gotten the Poet's Discount on erasers ever since!

When I write poetry, I'm not working. I'm playing. Whenever my author husband (Roderick Townley – go find his magical books!) and I travel to schools to talk about writing, we give out pencils engraved with this sentence: *The page is a playground.* That's how I think of the page – a place to run around and fall and hang upside down and generally galumph. It's messy and fun (you can't have one without the other).

Wyatt Townley is Poet Laureate of Kansas emerita and the author of six books. Two of her favorites are *Rewriting the Body* (Stephen F. Austin University Press, 2018) and *The Afterlives of Trees* (Woodley Press, 2011). Her work has been read on NPR and published in journals ranging from *North American Review* to *Paris Review*, *Yoga Journal* to *Scientific American*. Commissioned poems hang in libraries including the Space Telescope Science Institute, home of the Hubble.

A Poem by Wyatt Townley

The thing about poetry is that it is always there for you. People come and people go. Weather comes and weather goes. Whether we are readers or writers, poetry is always there for us. Its porchlight is always on.

KNOWING THE DIFFERENCE

The porchlight is on
its gold pours down
around your ankles

it follows you up the curve of night
slides through rows of corn
behind the parking lot

and when you have forgotten

the porchlight is on
the glossy black back
of the waterbug by the welcome mat

on the soundless
harp of the spider
behind the downspout

when you have not found what you had

to lose and your steps
are slow with doubt
the porchlight is on   look down

at your old shoes gleaming
you're the door you're
the difference between in and out

From the book *Rewriting the Body* (Stephen F. Austin State University Press, 2018).

A Word Ladder by Timothy Rasinski

In a word ladder game, lead students from one word to the next by adding, subtracting, or changing one or a few letters from the previous word. Start at the top and work toward the bottom.

1 Porch	An open platform with a roof that serves as the back or front entrance of a house.
2 Perch	A freshwater fish. Change 1 letter.
3 Parch	To make very dry by heating. Change 1.
4 Park	A place for picnics and play. Replace last 2 letters with 1.
5 Pack	How you put your clothes in a suitcase. Change 1.
6 Pick	To choose; also a sharp, pointed tool used for digging or breaking up rocks or other hard substances. Change 1.
7 Sick	Not well; feeling ill. Change 1.
8 Sit	What you do in a chair. Replace last 2 letters with 1.
9 Sight	Another word for the sense of vision. Add 2.
10 Light	Not heavy. Also, what the sun produces besides heat. Change 1.

4

List of Suggested Books to Read

In addition to the 40 poems provided by the poets in our book, we are proud to include this additional list of 162 titles that the poets themselves sent us to pass along to you. With one or two exceptions, these are all books of poems, primarily for grades 3–5. There aren't many lists like this, so we think this concluding chapter is quite a resource.

You'll see that some poets suggested further reading from their own work, while others included books they admire that are written or edited by others. Although there may be a handful of duplications, it's clear that poets read widely according to the range of their interests. You'll find additional diversity represented in the books they like and suggest for your students.

Allan Wolf

The Gift of the Broken Tea Cup: Poems of Mindfulness, Meditation, and Me by Allan Wolf. Candlewick Press, 2025.
How to Tantrum Like a Champion: Ten Small Ways to Temper Big Feelings by Allan Wolf. Candlewick Press, 2024.
Behold Our Magical Garden: Poems Fresh from a School Garden by Allan Wolf. Candlewick Press, 2022.
No Buddy Like a Book by Allan Wolf. Candlewick Press, 2021.

The Day the Universe Exploded My Head: Poems that Take You into Space and Back Again by Allan Wolf. Candlewick Press, 2019.

Betsy Franco

A Poke in the I. Selected by Paul B. Janeczko. Candlewick Press, 2001.
Welcome to the Wonder House by Rebecca Kai Dotlich and Georgia Heard. Wordsong, 2023.
Counting in Dog Years and Other Sassy Math Poems by Betsy Franco. Candlewick Press, 2022.
Bees, Snails, & Peacock Tails by Betsy Franco. Margaret K. McElderry Books, 2008.
Wishes, Lies, and Dreams: Teaching Children to Write Poetry by Kenneth Koch and Ron Padgett. Random House Inc., 1970.

Charles Ghigna

The Father Goose Treasury of Poetry: 101 Poems for Children by Charles Ghigna. Schiffer, 2023.
Bound to Dream: An Immigrant Story by Charles Ghigna. Schiffer, 2024.
The Magic Box: A Book of Opposites by Charles Ghigna. Schiffer, 2024.
Love Is Everything by Charles Ghigna. Schiffer, 2021.
A Poem Is a Firefly by Charles Ghigna. Schiffer, 2021.

Charles Waters

National Geographic Book of Animal Poetry: 200 Poems with Photographs That Squeak, Soar, and Roar! Edited by J. Patrick Lewis. National Geographic Kids; Illustrated edition, 2012.
Under the Mesquite by Guadalupe García McCall. Lee & Low Books, 2013.
Be a Bridge by Irene Latham and Charles Waters. Illustrated by Nabila Adani. Carolrhoda/Lerner, 2022.
Mascot by Charles Waters and Traci Sorell. Charlesbridge, 2023.
The Mistakes That Made Us: Confessions from Twenty Poets. Selected by Irene Latham and Charles Waters. Illustrated by Mercè López. Carolrhoda/Lerner, 2024.

David L. Harrison

Wild Brunch: Poems About How Creatures Eat by David L. Harrison. Charlesbridge, 2024.
A Tree Is a Community by David L. Harrison. Holiday House, 2024.
The Dirt Book: Poems About Animals that Live Beneath Our Feet by David L. Harrison. Holiday House, 2023.
After Dark: Poems About Nocturnal Animals by David L. Harrison. Wordsong, 2020.
Now You See Them, Now You Don't: Poems About Creatures That Hide by David L. Harrison. Charlesbridge, 2016.

Eileen Spinelli

Birdie by Eileen Spinelli. Eerdmans Books for Young Readers, 2019.
Thankful by Eileen Spinelli, illustrated by Archie Preston. Zonderkidz, 2015.
The Best Story by Eileen Spinelli, illustrated by Anne Wilsdorf. Dial Books for Young Readers, 2008.
Someday by Eileen Spinelli, illustrated by Rosie Winstead. Dial Books for Young Readers, 2007.
When You Are Happy by Eileen Spinelli, illustrated by Geraldo Valerio. Simon and Schuster Books for Young Readers, 2006.

Ellen Hopkins

School People, edited by Lee Bennett Hopkins. Wordsong, 2018.
Hate That Cat by Sharon Creech. HarperCollins, 2008.
Brown Girl Dreaming by Jacqueline Woodson. Nancy Paulsen Books, 2016.
Closer to Nowhere by Ellen Hopkins. Nancy Paulsen Books, 2020.
What About Will by Ellen Hopkins. Nancy Paulsen Books, 2023.

Eric Ode

Otters, Snails and Tadpole Tails: Poems from the Wetlands by Eric Ode. Kane Miller Books, 2019.
Stop That Poem! by Eric Ode. Kane Miller Books, 2021.

Out of Wonder by Kwame Alexander, Chris Colderley, and Marjory Wentworth. Candlewick Press, 2017.
A Festival for Frogs by Kenn Nesbitt. Purple Room Publishing, 2024.

Georgia Heard

Welcome to the Wonder House by Rebecca Kai Dotlich and Georgia Heard. Wordsong, Astra Books for Young Readers, 2023.
My Thoughts Are Clouds: Poems for Mindfulness by Georgia Heard. Roaring Brook Press, 2021.
Boom! Bellow! Bleat! Animal Poems for Two Or More Voices by Georgia Heard. Wordsong, Astra Books for Young Readers, 2023.
Falling Down the Page: A Book of List Poems by Georgia Heard. Roaring Brook Press, 2011.
For Teachers: Awakening the Heart (2nd edition) by Georgia Heard. Heinemann, 2024.

Greg Pincus

This Is Just to Say: Poems of Apology and Forgiveness by Joyce Sidman. Clarion Books, 2014.
Mirror, Mirror: A Book of Reverso Poems by Marilyn Singer. Dutton Books for Young Readers, 2010.
Mascot by Charles Waters and Traci Sorell. Charlesbridge, 2023.
A Poke in the I, selected by Paul B. Janeczko. Candlewick Press, 2001.
African Acrostics: A Word in Edgeways by Avis Harley. Candlewick Press, 2012.

Heidi E.Y. Stemple

Queer and Fearless: Poems Celebrating the Lives of LGBTQ+ Heroes by Rob Sanders, illustrated by Harry Woodgate. Penguin Workshop, 2024.
Tap Dancing on the Roof: Sijo (Poems) by Linda Sue Park, illustrated by Istvan Banyai. Clarion Books, 2015.
Thirteen Ways of Looking at a Black Boy by Tony Medina and 13 Artists. Penny Candy Books, 2018.

Your One and Only Heart by Rajani LaRocca, MD, illustrated by Lauren Paige Conrad. Dial Books, 2023.

Yuck You Suck: Poems About Animals That Sip, Slurp, Suck by Jane Yolen and Heidi E.Y. Stemple, illustrated by Eugenia Nobati. Millbrook Press, 2022.

Irene Latham

Can I Touch Your Hair? Poems of Race, Mistakes, and Friendship by Irene Latham and Charles Waters. Carolrhoda, 2018.

Dictionary for a Better World: Poems, Quotes, and Anecdotes from A to Z by Irene Latham and Charles Waters. Carolrhoda, 2020.

This Poem is a Nest by Irene Latham. WordSong, 2020.

The Museum on the Moon: The Curious Objects on the Lunar Surface by Irene Latham. Bushel & Peck Books (Moonshower), 2023.

The Proper Way to Meet a Hedgehog and Other How-to Poems, edited by Paul B. Janeckzo. Candlewick Press, 2019.

Jane Yolen

In and Out the Window by Jane Yolen, illustrated by Cathrin Peterslund. Philomel Books, 2024.

The Poetry of Science: The Poetry Friday Anthology for Science Kids by Sylvia Vardell and Janet Wong, illustrated by Frank Ramspott and Bug Wang. Pomelo Books, 2015.

Voice of Freedom Fannie Lou Hamer: Spirit of the Civil Rights Movement by Carole Boston Weatherford, illustrated by Ekua Holmes. Candlewick Press, 2015.

Nana and Me: Special Poems for Just Us by Jane Yolen, illustrated by Sejung Kim. Moonshower, 2023.

Woke: A Young Poet's Call to Justice by Mahogany L. Browne with Elizabeth Acevedo and Olivia Gatwood, illustrated by Theodore Taylor III. Roaring Brook Press, 2020.

Janet Wong

Great Morning! Poems for School Leaders to Read Aloud by Sylvia Vardell and Janet Wong. Pomelo Books, 2018.

Hop to It: Poems to Get You Moving by Sylvia Vardell and Janet Wong. Pomelo Books, 2020.
Knock on Wood: Poems about Superstitions by Janet S. Wong. McElderry/Simon & Schuster, 2003.
The Poetry Friday Anthology for Celebrations by Sylvia Vardell and Janet Wong. Pomelo Books, 2015.
Twist: Poems about Yoga by Janet S. Wong. McElderry/Simon & Schuster, 2007.

Joseph Bruchac

A Beginner's Guide to Japanese Haiku: Major Works by Japan's Best-Loved Poets by William Scott Wilson. Tuttle Publishing, 2022.
A Poetry Handbook: A Prose Guide to Understanding and Writing Poetry by Mary Oliver. Ecco, 1994.
The Poetry Home Repair Manual: Practical Advice for Beginning Poets by Ted Kooser. University of Nebraska Press, 2005.
Voices of the People by Joseph Bruchac. Reycraft, 2022.

Joyce Sidman

Dear Treefrog by Joyce Sidman. Houghton Mifflin Harcourt, 2021.
Firefly July: A Year of Very Short Poems, edited by Paul Janeczko. Candlewick Press, 2014.
Lion of the Sky: Haiku for All Seasons by Laura Purdie Salas. Millbrook Press, 2019.
Push-Pull Morning: Dog-Powered Poems About Matter and Energy by Lisa Westberg Peters. Wordsong, 2023.
Winter Bees and Other Poems of the Cold by Joyce Sidman. Houghton Mifflin Harcourt, 2014.

Kalli Dakos

They Only See the Outside by Kalli Dakos. Magination Press, 2021.
Recess in the Dark: Poems from the Far North by Kalli Dakos. DC Canada Education Publishing, 2019.

Happy Birthday, Belly Button by Kalli Dakos. Amicus Ink, 2023.
My Story Friend by Kalli Dakos. Magination Press, 2021.
If You're Not Here, Please Raise Your Hand: Poems About School by Kalli Dakos. Simon and Schuster, 1990.

Kate Coombs

Today I Am a River by Kate Coombs. Sounds True, 2023.
Breathe and Be: A Book of Mindfulness Poems by Kate Coombs. Sounds True, 2017.
Water Sings Blue by Kate Coombs. Chronicle Books, 2012.
All the Small Poems and Fourteen More by Valerie Worth. Square Fish (reprint), 1996.
The Great Frog Race and Other Poems by Kristine O'Connell George. Clarion Books, 1997.

Kenn Nesbitt

My Head Has a Bellyache: And More Nonsense for Mischievous Kids and Immature Grown-Ups by Chris Harris. Little, Brown Books for Young Readers, 2023.
Hard-Boiled Bugs for Breakfast: And Other Tasty Poems by Jack Prelutsky. Greenwillow Books, 2023.
Up Verses Down: Poems, Paintings, and Serious Nonsense by Calef Brown. Henry Holt and Co., 2019.
An Elephant Is Sitting in My Bathtub: Seriously Silly & Surprising Poems by Eric Ode. Deep Rooted Music, 2024.
Eating My Words: And 128 Other Poems by Brian P. Cleary. Millbrook Press, 2024.

Laura Purdie Salas

BookSpeak! Poems About Books. Poems by Laura Purdie Salas, illustrations by Josée Bisaillon. Clarion Books, 2011.
In the Middle of the Night: Poems from a Wide-Awake House. Poems by Laura Purdie Salas, illustrations by Angela Matteson. Wordsong, 2019.

In the Wild. Poems by David Elliott, illustrations by Holly Meade. Candlewick, 2013.
Lion of the Sky: Haiku for All Seasons. Poems by Laura Purdie Salas, illustrations by Mercé López. Millbrook Press, 2019.
Snowman - Cold = Puddle: Spring Equations. Poems by Laura Purdie Salas, illustrations by Micha Archer. Charlesbridge, 2019.
This Is Just to Say: Poems of Apology and Forgiveness. Poems by Joyce Sidman, illustrations by Pamela Zagarenski. Clarion Books, 2014.

Lesléa Newman

I Can Be… ME! by Lesléa Newman. Lee & Low, 2023.
The Fairest in the Land by Lesléa Newman. Abrams Books for Young Readers, 2023.
The Babka Sisters by Lesléa Newman. Kar-Ben Books, 2023.
Joyful Song: A Naming Story by Lesléa Newman. Levine/Querido, 2024.
Like Father, Like Son by Lesléa Newman. Abrams Books for Young Readers, 2024.

Marilyn Singer

Mirror Mirror: A Book of Reverso Poems by Marilyn Singer. Dial Books, 2010.
Follow Follow: A Book of Reverso Poems by Marilyn Singer. Dial Books, 2013.
Echo Echo: Reverso Poems about Greek Myths by Marilyn Singer. Dial Books, 2016.
Feel the Beat: Dance Poems that Zing from Salsa to Swing by Marilyn Singer. Dial Books, 2017.
Follow the Recipe: Poems About Imagination, Celebration, and Cake by Marilyn Singer. Dial Books, 2020.

Marjorie Maddox

A Crossing of Zebras: Animal Packs in Poetry by Marjorie Maddox, illustrated by Philip Huber. Reprinted by Wipf and Stock, 2019.
How Can I Look It Up When I Don't Know How It's Spelled? Spelling Mnemonics and Grammar Tricks by Marjorie Maddox. Kelsay Books, 2024.

I'm Feeling Blue, Too! by Marjorie Maddox, illustrated by Philip Huber. Wipf and Stock, 2020.
Inside Out: Poems on Writing and Reading Poems with Inside Exercises by Marjorie Maddox. Kelsay Books, 2020.
Rules of the Game: Baseball Poems by Marjorie Maddox, illustrated by John Sandford. Reprinted by Wipf and Stock, 2019.

Mary Lee Hahn

For teachers:

Poems Are Teachers by Amy Ludwig VanDerwater. Heinemann, 2018.

For classrooms and libraries:

The Museum on the Moon: The Curious Objects on the Lunar Surface by Irene Latham. Bushel & Peck Books (Moonshower), 2023.
Push-Pull Morning: Dog-Powered Poems About Matter and Energy by Lisa Westberg Peters. Penguin Random House, 2023.
National Geographic's The Poetry of US, edited by J. Patrick Lewis. National Geographic, 2018.
Imperfect: Poems About Mistakes, edited by Tabatha Yeatts. History House Publishers, 2018.

Maryfrances Wagner

Solving for X by Maryfrances Wagner. Spartan, 2019.
Red Silk by Maryfrances Wagner. BkMk Press, 2022 (Reprint).
The Immigrants' New Camera by Maryfrances Wagner. Spartan, 2018.
Ship of Fool by William Trowbridge. Red Hen, 2011.
Call Me Fool by William Trowbridge. Red Hen, 2022.

Matt Forrest Esenwine

The Thing to Remember About Stargazing by Matt Forrest Esenwine. Tilbury House, 2022.
Flashlight Night by Matt Forrest Esenwine. Astra Young Readers, 2017.
Don't Ask a Dinosaur by Matt Forrest Esenwine. POW! Kids Books, 2018.

I Am Today by Matt Forrest Esenwine. POW! Kids Books, 2022.
A Universe of Rainbows: Multicolored Poems for a Multicolored World, edited by Matt Forrest Esenwine. Eerdmans, 2025.

Nancy Bo Flood

We Rise, We Resist, We Raise Our Voices, edited by Wade Hudson & Cheryl Willis Hudson, 2018.
Give Me Back My Bones! by Kim Norman, illustrated by Bob Kolar. Candlewick Press, 2020.
Walking on Earth & Touching the Sky: Poetry and Prose by Lakota Youth at Red Cloud Indian School, edited by Timothy McLaughlin, paintings by S.D. Nelson. 2012.
Honey, I Love and Other Love Poems by Eloise Greenfield, pictures by Diane and Leo Dillon. 1978.
What Is a Friend? edited by Sylvia Vardell and Janet Wong. Pomelo Books, 2022.

Nikki Grimes

A Pocketful of Poems by Nikki Grimes. Clarion, 2001.
A Walk in the Woods by Nikki Grimes. Holiday House, 2023.
Poems in the Attic by Nikki Grimes. Lee & Low, 2015.
Southwest Sunrise by Nikki Grimes. Bloomsbury, 2020.
Thanks a Million by Nikki Grimes. Greenwillow, 2006.

Nile Stanley

Creating Readers with Poetry by Nile Stanley. Capstone Publishing, 2004.
Performance Literacy Through Storytelling by Nile Stanley and Brett Dillingham. Capstone Publishing, 2009.

Renée LaTulippe

When Green Becomes Tomatoes by Julie Fogliano, illustrated by Julie Morstad. Roaring Brook Press, 2016.

Legacy: Women Poets of the Harlem Renaissance by Nikki Grimes, various illustrators. Bloomsbury Children's Books, 2021.
All the Small Poems and Fourteen More by Valerie Worth, illustrated by Natalie Babbitt. Farrar Straus & Giroux, 1994.
The Crab Ballet by Renée M. LaTulippe, illustrated by Cécile Metzger. Abrams, 2022.
A Suitcase of Seaweed and More by Janet Wong. Pomelo Books, 2019.

Sandy Asher (Sandra Fenichel Asher)

Jesse and Grace: A Best Friend's Story by Sandra Fenichel Asher. Dramatic Publishing, 2010.
Somebody Catch My Homework by Sandra Fenichel Asher. Dramatic Publishing, 2004.
Heart to Heart: New Poems Inspired by Twentieth-Century American Art, edited by Jan Greenberg. Harry N. Abrams, Inc., 2001.
The Poetry Friday Anthology for Celebrations by Sylvia Vardell and Janet Wong. Pomelo Books, 2015.

Sylvia Vardell

A World Full of Poems selected by Sylvia Vardell. DK Books, 2020.
Countdown to Summer: A Poem for Every Day of the School Year by J. Patrick Lewis. Little, Brown, 2009.
Days to Celebrate: A Full Year of Poetry, People, Holidays, History, Fascinating Facts, and More selected by Lee Bennett Hopkins. Greenwillow, 2005.
Poetry Aloud Here 2: Sharing Poetry with Children (2nd edition) by Sylvia Vardell. American Library Association, 2014.
This Same Sky: A Collection of Poems from Around the World selected by Naomi Shihab Nye. Four Winds Press, 1992.

Ted Kooser

Marshmallow Clouds by Ted Kooser and Connie Wanek. Candlewick Press, 2023.
Cotton Candy: Poems Dipped Out of the Air by Ted Kooser. University of Nebraska Press, 2022.

Timothy Rasinski

Partner Poems and Word Ladders for Building Foundational Literacy Skills – Grades K-2 by David L. Harrison, Timothy Rasinski, and Mary Jo Fresch. Scholastic, 2022.

Partner Poems and Word Ladders for Building Foundational Literacy Skills – Grades 1–3 by David L. Harrison, Timothy Rasinski, and Mary Jo Fresch. Scholastic, 2022.

Daily Word Ladders: Grades K–1, 1–2, 2–4, 4–6 by Timothy Rasinski. Scholastic, 2012.

Wyatt Townley

The Great Good Thing by Roderick Townley. Simon & Schuster (Atheneum), 2001. New print edition (with new cover!) for its twenty-fifth anniversary in 2026!

The Miraculous Journey of Edward Tulane by Kate DiCamillo. Candlewick Press, 2006.

The Princess and the Goblin by George MacDonald. First published in 1871. Republished by Everyman's Library (Knopf), 1993.

Wet Cement: A Mix of Concrete Poems by Bob Raczka. Roaring Brook Press, 2016.

Miss Rumphius by Barbara Cooney. Penguin Random House (originally The Viking Press), 1982.

Made in the USA
Monee, IL
03 May 2026